Imperfectly
One

Growing together to find real love, grateful hearts and the
meaning of One.

A Free Gift for You
No Catch.

Through the years, we've has spent thousands of hours creating resources and materials to equip, empower and encourage you.

We think right now is a time we can all use a little hope. Can we send you one of our resources for free?

And by free, we really mean free (no required donation or shipping fee). Just tell us where to send it and we'll get it out to you.

God bless you!

If you want me to send you your free gift, just go to:

https://victormarx.com/gift/

Acknowledgements

My thanks to Julie Neils for her editorial suggestions and guidance on this project.

Kelsey Hulgan and Marsha Tohill, thank you for your editing skills.

To my husband of 31 years...

Twelve years into our marriage I started memorizing Proverbs 31. Little did I realize how deeply those verses would affect my soul. It's those words of life that sprang up a new commentary in my mind about what it really means to be a Proverbs 31 Woman.

This kind of woman is a standout. She understands her value and her influence in her world. She uses her life to bless those around her, to give life and value. She is not moved by culture's ideas or rhetoric on what makes a woman. She draws her value from her Creator, and she walks in it. She knows how important her role is to her family and doesn't take it lightly. Her husband depends on her and can always count on her. He trusts her implicitly and nurtures that trust. Though many things beckon for her attention, she stays focused on those that hold eternal value. She educates herself to remain relevant, she protects herself from the frivolous and ever-changing fads. Her study of God's word fortifies her mind and gives her discernment for the day's events. This woman is not perfect, but she doesn't settle for mediocrity, and she strives to be all that her Lord and Savior created her to be.

I can't think of a better way to celebrate our 31st anniversary than to reflect on Proverbs 31. My prayer is to become a fraction of this woman, to bring to life all the aspects of who she is and to bless you, my Victor, with the life-giving qualities of this type of person.

I thank you for always encouraging me to be my best, to see my value as God sees me, to understand the power and influence of my words.

You make me want to live as a Proverbs 31 Woman.

Sharing our life together as ONE is and always will be the best part of life.
I love you, my Victor!

Happy 31st Anniversary

- Eileen

Table of Contents

Introduction

Sitting at our favorite place in all the earth, looking across the table at my husband with a gentle smile on his face, memories flood my soul. Suddenly, I'm transported back to our wedding day, my heart so full of love and excitement, the surreal realization that this is really happening is settling in. We're standing at the altar looking into each other's eyes, knowing we share the same anticipation of what lies ahead of us. The joy I felt to spend the rest of my life with this man that I loved was uncontainable.

His question brought me back to our table. "How could 30 years go by so fast?" We agreed the moment we said "I do" felt as though it happened yesterday. I didn't want our time there to end, but reality called us back to being mom and dad.

We have so much history to look back on as one. So many incredible times together, and some very challenging ones that tested us as individuals and as a couple. Statistically, we should have not made it.
But we did.

We're living proof that marriage brings hardships and trials, the unwanted and the unexpected. Admittingly, at times I was tempted to give in and give up, but my heart knew that wasn't the answer. I'm so grateful we both chose to press through the hard times, the painful times. We would never have known or appreciated the sweet moments we know now had we chosen to give up.

There's a famous saying that "what doesn't kill you makes you stronger." Looking back, I wholeheartedly agree.

Our wedding was a dream. A beautiful December day in 1988, surrounded by family and friends there to witness and support the joyous occasion. Several years later, out of nowhere, it felt like our marriage was falling apart. My dream turned into a nightmare. How could our love for each other change so fast?

We found ourselves in an unrelenting cycle of fighting and frustration that seemed as though it would never end. We looked at one another and felt absolutely nothing. Life was beyond difficult. Many times, I thought to myself, "I did not sign up for this."

Desperately wanting better for each other and our marriage, but not knowing how to get it, Victor and I sought counseling from trusted friends and our pastor. They each gave us sound counsel and godly advice that was critical to preserving our marriage. I was also given advice from those who loved me and thought divorce was the best option. And though my heart was growing hard, neither Victor nor I ever considered divorce a viable option.

I hated living in that place of misery, constantly frustrated, angry, and bitter. I wanted to run, which was how I had always dealt with disappointment in the past, but I stayed.

I never thought I would be grateful for the hard, sometimes painful early years of our marriage, but today, I can say that I am truly grateful. I learned so much about myself. I learned just how selfish I was, just how immature I could be, and just how myopic my vision of life was. I never dreamed my marriage would be the source of some of my deepest wounds.

But where did I ever get the idea that marriage would be free of pain?

Marriage was never intended to be easy. How can it be when two people come together from different families, backgrounds, and childhoods? The idea is to walk through life together, growing, and being molded into one, in such a way that two people, living as one flesh, can endure some of life's hardest hits and come out of it stronger, together.

"For this reason, a man will leave his father and mother and cling to his wife, and the two will become one flesh." -Ephesians 5:31

Marriage is the only bond designed to last a lifetime. The sibling relationship was not created to last a lifetime. The parent/child relationship, one of the strongest of all bonds, was not created to last a lifetime. But marriage was.

God knew what He was doing when He created us and when He created marriage. He created man and woman — both uniquely different, yet both in His image. We were created to complement and complete one another, in order to help each other.

I see this design most clearly when I watch older couples. They communicate, often without words. The other day I saw an elderly couple in the grocery store. The wife pushed her shopping cart while the husband joyfully walked behind. She was the director of the cart, and her husband supported her role. It was obvious they were both happy and content as they have learned how to live and be together.

Whenever I see elderly couples walking down the street holding hands, I stop and wonder about their story. How many, if any, children do they have? Did they live through the Great Depression? What battles did they face together? Did they have a lot of money or face overwhelming debt? What illnesses have they lived through? What struggles did they face together?

To me, the beauty of it all is that they are still walking together, holding hands.

These precious couples inspire me. They are living proof that though life is tough, and it can sure take a toll on marriages, two committed, albeit imperfect people can arrive at the end of the journey with faithfulness, family, a grateful heart, and an intact marriage.

Unfortunately, this is not a message we hear very often. We seldom see this beautiful union that was created to last a lifetime held up as a standard. We see it struggling and competing against the overwhelming message that marriage between a man and a woman is outdated, archaic, and stifling. Sadly, marriage is increasingly seen as a throwaway institution.

So many young people are choosing to forego marriage altogether and just live together. Why? Is it about convenience or the fear of committing to one person for a lifetime? Have they seen the devastating effects of broken marriages and the collateral damage children now have to live with? Are they living with the collateral damage themselves?

The thought of giving yourself to another person for a lifetime is not celebrated, encouraged, or endorsed by many today.

I talked to a woman the other day who was living with her boyfriend. I asked her if they planned to get married, and she said she wasn't sure. I asked what motivation he had to propose if they were already sleeping together and suggested that she refrain from any further sex until he's ready to make the commitment to marry her.

I wonder how that conversation went.

Maybe you're in a similar situation. Maybe you and your live-in boyfriend are in a stagnant relationship. Maybe you and your spouse are in a cycle of fighting with no end in sight. If that is you, I pray you will find hope, truth and motivation within the pages of this book.

The odds were certainly not in our favor on that December day when Victor and I made our vows.

As individuals, we separately experienced childhoods marked by dysfunctional home lives, the pain of divorced parents, and broken homes. As a couple, we faced the tragic effects of childhood sexual abuse, PTSD, separation, and many other challenges. At one point, Victor, who was a martial arts instructor at the time, completely tore his hamstring. This physical trauma allowed the emotional childhood trauma to surface that he had tried to hide for years. I watched my husband unravel as his ability to provide for our family was seemingly gone in the blink of an eye. With symptoms that mimic bipolar disorder, he was medicated for and diagnosed with this condition. What came next were years of psychiatry visits, a plethora of medications, and many more challenges for the two of us to face.

Any one of these things could have ended our marriage. We could have been a statistic. But we made a promise to each other and to God on that exciting winter day in 1988 — a day filled with the joyful anticipation of being husband and wife, when we sensed the supernatural presence of the Holy Spirit envelop, bind, and seal us together as a couple. Though we could not have possibly known what our future held, we believed God had brought us together for something much bigger than just the two of us. Through it all, He has walked with us every step of the way and enabled us to keep that promise.

With Him, all things are possible.

Chapter 1
The Beginning of Us

Victor grew up in a very abusive environment. He had multiple stepfathers, lived in 17 different homes, went to 14 different schools, and was exposed to many traumatic events as a small boy. He went to several different churches and was even enrolled in a Christian school at one point, but he felt that God must not love him because of all the bad things that had been allowed to happen to him. It wasn't until after he left home to join the Marines that he started going to church.

Right before he got out of the Marines, Victor submitted his life to Christ and came into a personal relationship with Jesus. From that point, he jumped into ministry headfirst. He was so eager to do whatever God wanted. So much so that he showed up at his Southern California church and asked to mow the lawn or take out the garbage--whatever needed doing. After some time, the church staff saw potential in this enthusiastic, charismatic 21-year-old who had an ability to connect with people, especially young people, and put him to work. They made him the junior high school pastor and his first order of business was to lead a Bible study group. Because there weren't enough classrooms to go around, his group met in a school bus!

Eager to serve and contribute, Victor, a martial arts expert, felt led to start a karate class. The pastor allowed him to announce his plans from the pulpit, and that same day more than 100 people signed up. Within a week, he was teaching a class with over 120 people! With karate classes that were bearing much fruit in the lives of the young people he served, Victor had found his calling. He started thinking more and more about finding a wife.

Not surprisingly, some of the young women in the church were already eyeing him. He dated one or two in hopes that a relationship would turn into marriage, but they didn't. One woman even declared that God had told her she was going to marry Victor and move to Louisiana with him. Some older women in the church had strong opinions about his relational status as well, and a few issued a, "Thus says the Lord, you are to marry this gal," word of prophecy. Such heavy-handed decrees only added to Victor's confusion, as did his insecurities about his past. He began to think that he would have to marry someone even if he didn't love her, because of the bad things he had done.

That's when I entered the picture.

I was a fitness instructor and one of my students invited me to her church. She was a beautiful young mother with the most adorable baby girl that grabbed my heart the first time I saw her. She was friendly and full of life, and she invited me to join her at church several times. Each time, I politely declined. I had just returned from a job in Italy and was doing pretty well for myself. I really didn't think I needed church. I worked hard. I lived in the moment. Making money was the most important thing in my life and as far as that was concerned, I was successful.

As far as religion, I didn't have a foundation to speak of. My philosophy was that a sound body and a sound mind were all I needed in this life. To me, God was a distant being, someone or something that was very impersonal. I had no desire to go to church. Nonetheless, my student, Trish, kept inviting me, and finally I gave in.

The small, rustic church with wooden pews and floors was full that Wednesday evening. Trish was a member of the worship team, and her talent surprised me. I had no idea she could sing like that! Her sincerity, as well as others in the church singing with eyes closed and hands lifted into the air, moved me deeply. Nothing I experienced in my life had prepared me for this. I found myself going back on

Wednesday nights, and also on Sunday mornings. I didn't know why, but I felt compelled to go. For the first time in my life, I heard the Bible being taught in such a way that it made me want to learn more.

Trish introduced me to the two things that would most influence the rest of my life--the Christian church and my future husband, Victor. One of the first things I noticed about this young guy who was fresh out of the Marines was his smile. He had a great smile, very kind eyes, and a friendly demeanor. However, in the beginning, Victor was far more excited about getting to know me than I was about getting to know him. So much so, I discovered much later, that he had already told the Lord, "I'll marry that one!"

Victor was growing in his new faith and fervently praying for my salvation, as I was not yet a Christian. But that all changed one Sunday morning. Since the very first time I stepped foot into that church, I felt there was something special that kept me coming back again and again (and no, it wasn't Victor). I just couldn't name it. Well, this particular Sunday marked the fourth month of me coming to this church. Four months of hearing the Bible taught, and four months of hearing over and over, again and again, how much God and Jesus loved me. And though I typically made a habit of sitting in the back row and making a beeline for the door at the conclusion of the service, that Sunday I was off my routine and subsequently out of my comfort zone. There I was in the front row. The singer's songs and lyrics moved me deeply as she asked if anyone wanted to receive Jesus Christ as their Savior. "Why wait until tomorrow?" she pressed. It seemed she was speaking directly to me. Tears started streaming down my face, my heart pounding in my chest. My emotions were well beyond my control; I had no idea what was happening to me. I hated feeling out of control. For the first time in my life, I sensed my need for Jesus. It was as if He was right there, speaking directly to my heart, asking me to trust Him. I knew

I was without Him. I knew I wanted Him. I wept as I surrendered my life to Him.

Not long after that pivotal day, I started attending Victor's karate class. He was an excellent teacher and so very funny. He always made me laugh. We appreciated each other's passion for fitness and martial arts. And though I was working full-time as a physical therapist assistant, going to school and teaching fitness classes at two health clubs, when Victor asked me to start teaching fitness classes at his dojo karate school (a gym focusing on martial arts), I decided to give it a try. As an entrepreneur, I couldn't pass up the opportunity to make more money. It was then that Victor and I began to see more of each other, hanging out after class and eating together after church.

Even then, he still wasn't necessarily a romantic contender in my mind.

One afternoon while sunbathing with a girlfriend, I heard a voice in my head say, "You are going to marry Victor." I said out loud, "What?" We were just friends, but that was it. And I wasn't interested in more — with him or anyone else for that matter. Just the idea of dating exhausted me. Confused and upset, I told my friend what I heard. She assured me that I didn't have to marry him. What a relief! I would later find that Victor, however, had not only heard God tell him I was going to be his wife, but he had also written it down in his journal, just to be sure.

Not too long after that experience, I threw a baby shower for a friend at my house. Victor came and brought his dad. After the party, his dad went into the kitchen and started doing dishes while Victor and I stayed in the living room. As a white belt in his karate school, I wanted to learn more of the requirements necessary to get my next stripe. Victor happily taught me the requirements. As he was teaching me, I noticed a change start to happen in my heart. I genuinely began to see him differently.

As I spent more time around Victor, I noticed things that stood out from the other men I had dated. Above all, he was a gentleman. I remember hearing him speak to his mother on the phone, saying "Yes, ma'am," and "No, ma'am," kindly and easily, indicative of his great love and respect for her. He was also kind and very gentle. With few words, he made me feel valued and cherished. I also greatly admired his natural leadership skills. We spent many hours on the phone talking about anything and everything, sometimes until the wee hours of the morning. Recollecting our nightly conversations at work the next day gave me the energy and motivation to make it through the day.

Once we were an item, things went pretty fast. I'd never had someone care so much about me in the way that Victor did. It was so different from previous relationships, but my life was also much different now. I had a relationship with this man who I really cared about, and I had a relationship with Jesus, the One who changed my life.

Three months after we started dating, we went to Lake Arrowhead, California to perform a karate demo at a youth conference and Victor took me to a scenic overlook called Strawberry Peak. High up in the mountains with pine trees everywhere, the view was breathtaking. As we were walking, Victor plucked a long weed out of the ground, twisted it into the shape of a ring, and knelt down on one knee.

"Eileen, will you spend the rest of your life with me?"

At first, I didn't think he was actually serious. He caught me completely off guard. Victor has a great sense of humor, and after all, he was proposing with a weed. I laughed nervously. Undeterred, he tried again. "Eileen, I want you to be my wife. Let's grow old together. Will you marry me?"

This time, I took him seriously and gave him my answer. "Yes!" It was a perfect moment — the culmination of our gradual and beautiful dating journey.

Just a little more than two years after we first met, we were married on a magical December day. I wore a majestic gown handmade by one of our friends: yards and yards of white satin fabric, a seven-foot train adorned with more than 2,000 handsewn pearls. I felt like a princess when I walked down the aisle. I met Victor, handsome as ever in his white tuxedo, at the altar, surrounded by our bridal party in their red satin dresses and black tuxedos. I couldn't believe we were getting married. This was it. This was our fairytale. One my heart had never really wanted until now.

That is the story of how we began. How the Lord crossed our paths, worked in our hearts, and brought us together. But the rest of the story is how we became one, and how we have remained one. How we have faced some of life's most impossible challenges — together.

To Think About: How did your story begin? In what ways were you and your spouse naive to the commitment you were making to each other? In what ways are you struggling in your marriage today? Pray for the Lord to give you clarity regarding the issues you face as we spend time together learning about His ultimate design for marriage in this book.

Chapter 2
Purity

The word purity has become so polarizing in our society. The very mention of the word makes people cringe and get very defensive. If you have chosen to remain sexually pure, you are certainly in the minority and will likely encounter many who do not understand your choice and may even mock you for it.

Before Victor and I became Christians, we were just like our peers and fell into the camp of not understanding why someone would choose to remain sexually pure. We thought that having sex with someone you were not married to was completely acceptable. If everyone does it, how could it be so wrong?

The truth is, we both suffered long-lasting emotional consequences as a result of being sexually promiscuous. God created sex and knew what was best for mankind when He put limitations on it. Doing so wasn't to withhold something good from us. Sex is a gift--the very best one when kept within the boundaries of marriage.

When Victor and I started dating, we committed to pursuing this relationship God's way. That meant no sex until our wedding night, and no sex with anyone else after. Ever. It was and continues to be so worth it.

Making this commitment to honor God and each other truly laid a solid foundation for our relationship. This was more than a morality issue for us--our character was being tested. Were we willing to put this desire in its proper place--for marriage--or would we give into the desires of our flesh that seemed so natural? These character issues--exhibiting honor and self-control--are key ingredients in marriage. If we could not honor one another and practice self-control before marriage, would it be a priority after?

Little did we know just how much we would need this solid foundation.

Our early years of marriage were tested on just about every front. We experienced the same kinds of stress as most couples, like finances, babies, loss of sleep, new jobs, moving, advances from other people, and job changes, to name a few. Because our intimacy was grounded in trust and believing what God says about sex and marriage, it became the glue that would hold us together when we started to feel strain. So many pressures had the potential to divide us, but I truly believe our intimacy held us together. It continues to be a strong pillar in our marriage today.

The choice to prioritize purity didn't cease when we got married. Purity is a concept that overflows into many areas of our lives, as individuals and as a couple.

The truth is that we live in a sex-saturated culture. Everything hinges on sex! It's all around us, beckoning our attention, acceptance, and tolerance. We can't go anywhere without being subjected to some form of explicit images or solicitation. Victor is solicited often when he travels. I'm still shocked at the open aggressiveness and forwardness of women today; it's as though conquering a married man is a highly valued prize to be won.

Victor was recently approached by a man and woman at a hotel where he was teaching at a mission conference. They approached him, striking up a conversation about our dog, Scout. The man showed Victor a photo of his dogs with a naked woman--the woman that was standing right next to Victor. The woman confessed that the photo wasn't very flattering of her. This couple was trying to solicit my husband! After hearing Victor say he was a grandfather, the man turned to the woman and said, "How would you like to do a grandfather?" Realizing what was going on, Victor began showing them photos of me, his wife, and explaining the high-risk mission work we do all over the world. When he ran into them again in the hotel lobby, he invited them both to church the next day where he was speaking. I bet they had never considered that this man they were soliciting was a preacher!

We don't get angry at people who do these kinds of things, but rather we have compassion toward the hearts of those who are caught up in this darkness.

Start Overs

Is it possible to have a healthy marriage if we have missed it in this area? Yes, it is! Make it your goal to stay pure from this point forward and give the past to the Lord. Only He can restore what was done and help you and your spouse have a healthy and honoring sex life. Don't follow the world's way of sex. You don't need porn or X-rated movies. You don't need to get cues or even ideas from other people, magazines, or friends. God's Word is good. Look at sex the way Solomon does in the book, Song of Solomon. He is very open and explicit in describing his relationship with his bride, so she is also very open in her passion and ideas for sexual intimacy. Communicate your desires to each other and keep your sex life pure and undefiled. Stay away from perversion of any kind--it will destroy the foundation of your marriage. Confess your sins to one another, keeping no record of wrongs and forgiving one another.

Do you ever wonder why the forces of darkness work so hard to tempt and discourage sexual purity before marriage, and then work so hard to divide and discourage couples from having sex in marriage? It's because sex in marriage represents the love and intentionality of God Almighty toward His most prized creation. The enemy of our souls cannot stand the fact that God created sexual intimacy with a purpose and for the pleasure of a man and a woman *in a holy union*. This union is so incredible that God Himself is actually present in the midst of it.

That's why we openly and eagerly share with young people, old people—really, anyone who will listen--that staying pure and keeping oneself for his or her future spouse is the best way to win this relentless battle. Following God's plan before marriage and His redemptive plan when mistakes are made will give you the best chance at creating and maintaining this sacred union for which we were truly created.

God's heart is for you to enjoy your oneness in marriage. If you are married, the most powerful thing you can do is forgive when you have been wronged. This only happens for me when I understand just how much God has forgiven and how much He continues to forgive me. I refuse to hold on to unforgiveness. Unforgiveness robs us and locks us in a prison of resentment and bitterness that further hardens our hearts. Victor and I have found that honest and open communication is the key to resolving these hurts and granting true forgiveness. Yes, the truth can cause pain, but truth and honesty are so very powerful. This kind of transparency can crush the enemy and his strategy against you and your marriage. If what you need to share with your spouse is difficult, pray over your conversation beforehand. Ask the Holy Spirit to prepare your heart, as well as your spouse's, so that your words will be received. Pray until you have peace.

If you are single, watch out for your emotions! They cannot be trusted, and so easily influence our hearts and our actions. Seek people who have gone through the battlefield in marriage and have come out stronger. Pray for your future spouse. Ask God to protect him from the world and its damaging mentality. Pray for yourself. Ask God to show you what you can't see. Ask Him to give you strength to remain pure and content during this season of your life. Finally, don't ever compromise and give in to what you know is wrong.

If you are single, save every part of yourself for your spouse before marriage. If you are married, let your spouse have all of you in marriage. War for it. Protect it. And then watch it develop into the beautiful union God designed it to be.

Don't set yourself up for failure by toying or flirting with temptation. You won't win. You are human, made of flesh and blood. Regardless of our intentions, without healthy, sustainable boundaries in place, chances are we'll cave. Find a friend who will help you stay on track and hold you accountable. Be deliberate and vigilant, stand strong and fight for purity in your marriage or purity in your singleness. It is honorable in the sight of the Lord.

Committing this part of our lives to God has strengthened us and given us a heart for the many who don't have the luxury of making this choice for themselves. Sadly, our travels around the world have shown this to be the case for so many innocent people.

Not long ago, Victor and I sensed the Lord leading us to rent a booth at the annual AVN Adult Entertainment Expo, also known as "the porn show," in Las Vegas. More than 500 porn stars were there, along with 25,000 attendees, and we hoped to be a source of light for so many people trapped in such darkness.

Going into this environment--the pit of our enemy's playground--was darker and more challenging than I thought it would be. My heart was overwhelmed with feelings of sadness for the beautiful young women who were caught up or trapped in this lifestyle, many with self-esteem the size of a gnat. Women were standing behind tables on display for others to come by and stare--to gawk and lust. When I looked into their eyes, I saw pain and emptiness. I saw them as children; their innocence ripped away from them. It broke my heart. It's easy to see how they might believe that this is all they're good for; for people to lust over them. I wanted to hug each one and tell them, "You're so much more than this. You are so valuable and so much more precious than you could ever know." One young woman looked to be 12 years old, as she posed next to her life-size poster. We caught her attention with our dog, Scout.

As she bent down to pet Scout, we had a moment to talk with her and tell her about our work with young women and children affected by trauma. She seemed as though she wanted to tell us something but stopped. We sensed that her pimp was close by, controlling her with his presence. We gave her Scout's card and walked away, deeply saddened. We keep her picture on our fridge and pray for her daily.

The sad truth is that this young woman is just one of many who are caught up in this destructive lifestyle—one that leads to utter despair. They often feel stuck, with no way out. Many commits suicide. In fact, one of the reasons we felt so compelled to go to this show was because four women in the industry had recently committed suicide.

In early 2015, we took our first trip to the Middle East, into Northern Iraq, to help young women who had been kidnapped, horribly abused, and forced to marry by ISIS, but were now free. Although no longer imprisoned, many were taking their lives, forever scarred and unable to forget the horrible abuse they experienced. As they shared in detail their stories with me, I was overwhelmed with such grief for these precious young women (each could have been my daughter). These young women will carry the scars of the horrific and senseless evil acts committed against them throughout their lives.

It doesn't matter what part of the world you live in; innocent people are the targets of those who have given themselves over to evil and perversion.

To see the ramifications of such abuse motivates us to be the voice, hands and feet of Jesus. We know God can heal these victims and renew their hearts and minds, but for many it causes devastating side effects--from promiscuity to drug and alcohol abuse to a lifetime of destructive relationships--and even suicide. Victims believe the lies that they're not valuable, or that God allowed these things to happen to them. Sadly, this often prevents them from coming to Him and believing just how much He loves them. He can and longs to heal them. He desires to set them free! Jesus came to heal the brokenhearted — that's His message to the world.

Whether your story is one of abuse or promiscuity, our God is in the business of healing, restoring, and making new. **We are living proof of this.**

To Think About: What are you doing to protect your sexual purity? What boundaries do you have in place that will help you stay sexually pure in marriage or before marriage?

Chapter 3
Words, Wounds & Weaknesses

"Sticks and stones may break my bones, but words will never hurt me." This was a popular saying when I was growing up and I can still hear the words being chanted on the playground. Unfortunately, this is so far from the truth. Our words can bring more pain and have the potential to last much longer than a broken bone. Trust me when I tell you that my heart echoed this sentiment early in my marriage, as I let hurtful words fly out of my mouth without giving thought to how they made my husband feel.

Proverbs 18:21 says, "The tongue has the power of life and death..." Talk about power. Truly, words create worlds of their own. What an opportunity we have as wives and husbands to use our words along with our actions, talents, wisdom, and insight to help strengthen the areas of our spouses' lives that need it.

Let's face it—we all have weaknesses and we each bring differences into our marriages: different backgrounds, families, experiences, wounds, skills, and even different senses of humor. Our weaknesses are no different.

Victor and I had our fair share of differences. I came into our marriage needing to prove and provide for myself, and not because Victor ever made me feel that I should. In fact, it was quite the contrary. It was a weakness of mine—a place in my heart where I didn't feel 100% safe with him. I always had a backup plan. There was always a red, flashing light in the back of my mind that said, "If something goes wrong, I need to be ready and able to provide for myself."

Why? Because years ago, someone had created a world for me with the power of her words.

When I was 15 years old, my twin sister and I lived in an apartment by ourselves as we completed our sophomore year in high school. Our mom's business didn't go quite as planned, and she had to move to another city to take a different job close to the end of our school year. Understandably, she didn't want to pull us out of school with only a couple of months before summer break. So, in this unconventional, temporary arrangement, my sister and I got to stay by ourselves in an apartment. We were in heaven! And the amazing thing was that we actually got ourselves up and out of the door to school every morning. Well, almost every morning.

After a month of living on our own, mom realized this wasn't the best situation for me and my sister. She asked a friendly neighbor if we could live with her and her family for a couple of weeks, just until school was out. One day, our neighbor friend asked me to go and ask the apartment manager a question. Eager to be of help, I set off to accomplish my mission.

When I knocked on the door, the manager opened it. She was an older woman who looked at me and shook her finger in my face. She said something to me that changed the way I thought of myself for years to come: "You are such an imposition."

I don't remember the question I asked. All I remember is the five words she said and the utter disdain with which she said them.

I made a vow that day that I would never be an imposition to anyone. Anyone. From that point on, I would make it on my own.

Like many inner vows, I wasn't fully aware of how that promise would seep into many areas of my life. But when we got married, boy did it rear its ugly head. It was hard for me to let Victor live out his God-given, natural desire to protect, provide and lead. Why? Because I needed to be in control. Being in control made me feel safe. The few times I did "allow" him to lead, I put up a pretty good fight. It was a struggle for both of us.

That inner vow I made so many years before was crippling our marriage. It was crippling Victor. In reality, it was crippling me as well.

But one day, God allowed something to happen that changed my heart.

I was pregnant with our first child and together, Victor and I were running our first martial arts and fitness center. I was making copies of a flier a few doors down from our dojo, where the owner made a rude comment to me. When I returned, Victor could see I was visibly upset. He asked me what had happened, and I told him. Within seconds, he was out the door marching toward the copy shop. Victor told the owner that he would not tolerate him talking down to or being rude to his wife.

Something wonderful happened in my heart when I watched my husband stand up for me. I felt a sense of security in my soul that I had never felt before. My husband was doing what was so natural for him — protecting his wife. I was immensely moved, watching his strength cover and empower me in a place where I was so weak and unsure of myself. I've never forgotten it.

Since that first time Victor stood up for me, there have been many times that he's shown protectiveness over me and our children. This is a natural drive in the heart of my husband. I believe God made men with this built-in protectiveness. It comes so naturally to them that they don't have to fabricate it. I know there are many men who don't allow this quality to surface, but I am so glad that my husband isn't afraid to live it out. I need his strength.

Just as Victor's strength covered me where I was weak, there have been other times where the situation has been reversed. And there have been many, many times where we relied on the strength of God alone, when ours was all but gone.

I remember one time very vividly. I found Victor—who is a 7th degree black belt and former Marine—crying out in terror and pain. He was having a flashback from his childhood of someone hurting him. It was more than he could handle and, in that moment, in Victor's mind it was as if the incident was happening all over again. He ran into a running shower and dropped to the floor with his knees pulled to his chest. "Please don't let them kill me! Please don't let them kill me!" he screamed.

I didn't know what to do. My heart hurt so deeply for my husband. Without thinking, I walked into the shower, fully clothed, knelt down next to Victor, and just held him. I cried with him and let him know everything was going to be ok.

Later Victor said, "I felt like God Almighty stepped into my pain and was holding me and letting me know how much He loved me."

The Lord allowed me to be there in Victor's hellish moment and gave me the strength to be His hands and heart to Victor, who desperately needed to tangibly feel the presence of God.

What a gift to be used by the Lord in this way.

There is no one, but you, who will ever fully see the wounds and weaknesses deep inside your spouse. A healthy marriage means that you can both feel safe, even when those imperfections are exposed. God has put you in a unique place to breathe life into those vulnerable places with your words, your actions, and most of all, with the Word of God. Allow God's strength to empower you both as you walk down this road together. In doing so, what is dull will become sharp, and what is weak will become strong. *Our words really do create worlds.*

To Think About: What world are you creating for your spouse with the words that you speak? What weaknesses does he have that you can help strengthen? What weaknesses do you have that he can bolster?

Chapter 4
Early Years, Early Lessons

Being young in our faith and newlyweds to boot sometimes made for a bumpy—albeit interesting—ride that taught us some important lessons in the early years of our marriage. These lessons and experiences steadied us for the ones to come.

I don't know how to explain our journey without acknowledging that God supernaturally enabled us to walk by faith and not by sight. If we had walked by sight, placing our faith in what we could see, we never would have made it. But in His faithful grace, God took us through each challenge, one at a time, allowing us to overcome our culture's incredible odds along the way.

For example, the world says, "Don't start a family until you have a decent savings account and own your own home." We had neither and four months into our marriage found out we were pregnant. Excited and overwhelmed, Victor and I chose not to dwell on how we were going to afford this little one, but on Who we could trust to provide for us. Victor was teaching karate at our recently opened martial arts and fitness center in California, while I taught aerobics and fitness classes. As self-employed business owners, we had no insurance.

We needed $2,200 to deliver our baby at the hospital. Weeks before our little one arrived, an anonymous gift of cash was delivered to our karate center. The amount? $2,200. God showed us over and over again that we could trust Him to provide for our needs. Sometimes, right down to the dollar.

Parenthood brought us so much joy. I was the youngest of eight children and I always loved holding other people's babies, but this time I had my very own. Our baby girl was such a beautiful gift from God. I couldn't believe she was ours; sometimes I would just stare at her and pinch myself! Since we owned our business, I would bring our daughter to work with me. And when Victor came home from teaching, he couldn't wait to spend time with his baby girl. We were a very happy little family.

Not long after our daughter was born, Victor began to sense the Lord wanting us to move to Louisiana. He had a deep desire to minister to the hearts of those he had grown up around in Cajun country. God confirmed this calling and opened the door for us to start a new church in a small city on the bayou. By that time, I was pregnant with our second child and we still didn't own a home, have health insurance, or a hefty savings account. I was nauseous around the clock, had a busy toddler to care for, and my mustard-seed-sized faith was being tested in a new way. Far from my California home, I longed for the comfort and support of friends and family, but God used this time to show me that He, and He alone, would be a firm foundation for me, my husband, our baby girl, and the next little one on the way.

To put food on the table, Victor took a job as a car salesman. While we looked for a place to live, we took up residence in a cockroach-infested hotel — not the ideal place to launch this new season of our ministry and family life, to say the least, but we made do. When Victor's first paycheck finally came, we rented an apartment and rejoiced, yet again, in God's provision.

Those were some tough days. At one point, we were so low on cash that we had no money to buy food. That same day we were surprised to find several bags of groceries left for us on our doorstep. God used a kind young woman from church to meet our need. Then, one month before our little one arrived, we were involved in a car accident, the impact of which was severe. Victor suffered from whiplash and because my pregnancy was so far along, we had to go to the hospital to make sure the baby and I were okay. Thankfully, a pastor friend let us use his car until we could get ours fixed. In each of these instances, God gave us the faith to trust in His ability to provide, and most of all, in His heart toward us and our everyday needs.

Little did we know, greater challenges to our faith were yet to come.

My first pregnancy and delivery had gone smoothly. The circumstances were ideal—our baby girl came right on time, the doctor and the hospital were close by, and my parents came to help out with the transition. My mom stayed with us for an entire week, which was such a blessing. I remember crying when she left because I truly didn't know how we would make it without her.

This time around, however, the situation was very different. My doctor was two-and-a-half-hours away. We didn't want to risk not making it to the hospital in time for delivery, so we chose to have a home birth. My concerned mother was not too keen on the idea and voiced her concern from thousands of miles away. And though I understood her concern, I told her I felt at peace about our decision. And I did. Soon after that conversation, we met with two local midwives who listened to our predicament and agreed to help us deliver our baby at home.

To our delight, our sweet baby boy was born on the Fourth of July, a week after his due date. We chose not to find out the gender during my pregnancy so that we could enjoy the surprise in the moment. Unbeknownst to me, Victor had quietly prayed, both that we would have a son, and that I would give birth at home. Not only did God answer his prayer, but He did so one day before Victor's 25th birthday. Our son was born in our home on Bayou Blue, just a couple of hours from where Victor had grown up. What a special birthday gift!

Seven weeks later, I was changing our little guy's diaper when I felt his skin. His little body was alarmingly hot, and I noticed that he was very lethargic. Sensing something was very wrong, we took our son to the hospital. We watched as our baby boy was strapped down, poked and prodded, his little frame hot to the touch and his face red from his cries. A test revealed he had developed spinal meningitis, a very serious and sometimes deadly condition. He was immediately quarantined.

"There are seven chances in ten that your son will die, be deaf or have severe physical disabilities from this illness," the doctor warned us. "A seventy percent chance," he resolved.

His diagnosis seemed hopelessly final, but in our hearts, we knew it was not.

Away from my family, scared and very much alone, I lay in the hospital bed with my son while he was fed intravenously. When able, I nursed him and prayed continuously that God would heal his little body. As hard as it was for him to leave us, Victor had to continue to work. As he drove from work to our home to the hospital and back, he continuously cried out to God, begging Him to have mercy on our son. While in his car, Victor turned on the radio and heard a preacher declare, "Today is your day for a miracle! A child needs a miracle and God is going to provide that miracle and heal that sick child. You must believe."

Victor received that as an answer from the Lord, and immediately drove to the hospital where I maintained my constant vigil and told me of the preacher's words. Minutes later, the doctor and nurse came into our room. "Mr. and Mrs. Marx," the doctor said, "Your son does not have spinal meningitis. Your son can go home now." We were in shock.

"Doctor, that's a miracle!" Victor yelled.

We thanked God and praised Him for healing our son, and though the doctor never acknowledged his sudden healing as a miracle, we knew it was. We took our baby home and within three days, he was completely healed. Through this ordeal, God taught us that His sovereign hand remains in control, even when things seem hopeless. No matter what man says, God always has the last word.

Eighteen months later, we felt our time in Louisiana was complete. We had two beautiful, healthy children and witnessed God do some incredible things in the small church that Victor pastored. Many young families were now attending the church and several people had received Christ. We witnessed the healing and restoration of a completely broken marriage and a father who was freed from his smoking addiction. We saw the faith of other couples grow as God provided for them, just as He had for us. Most of all, we watched in wonder to see the personal nature of God's care for each of us.

From the groceries on our doorstep, to the down-to-the-dollar hospital delivery fee, to the healing of our precious son, each miracle was a gift from the Lord to grow our faith. God enabled us to simply take Him at His Word in those early years, and I'm so glad we did. The journey would not have been nearly as sweet or full of adventure had we listened to culture and gone the "safe route."

From Louisiana, we packed up and headed back to California. In truth, I didn't care where we were going as long as it was out of Louisiana. I would miss the beautiful people and incredible food, but happily left the cockroaches, mosquitoes, and miserable humidity behind.

Victor started a little karate school in Lompoc, California—a little school that by God's grace eventually became one of the top five karate schools in America. Though we were comforted by the familiar surroundings of home, the next few years would prove to be a foreign, unsettling testing ground for our marriage.

To Think About: Can you remember times in your life where God was providing, protecting, and guiding you? It's important to remember these and write them down, so that you can look back and be encouraged when you're faced with a new trial. Take some time to write down those times and events where God intervened on your behalf.

Chapter 5
Honor

"Harooooold!" yelled a white-haired woman as she stood in the doorway of the men's restroom. My husband, who was speaking at an upscale hotel in Southern California, stood washing his hands at the sink. Victor looked around and said, "I don't think anyone's in here, ma'am."

Undeterred, she pushed her way through the door and made her way down the row of stalls. She paused at a lone, locked door and tried again. "Harold!" she commanded. Silence. A few moments later, the poor man on the other side of the door spoke, "I can assure you there is no Harold in here." Off she marched out of the men's room and into the hallway to look for her husband.

A few minutes later, Victor saw an elderly man walking out of the women's restroom. "That must be Harold," Victor laughed to himself.

I laughed, too, when I heard this story, but I cringed for poor Harold. Humiliation of any kind is rough, but humiliation at the hands of your spouse is brutal.

Overt acts of humiliation are a sign of dishonor in a relationship. Unfortunately, dishonor has become a common problem in our society and in many marriages today. In our 30 years of marriage, I have learned that honor is a two-way street. How I treat my husband makes a huge difference in how he treats me.

Honor used to be a pillar of our society. We were taught to honor the elderly, to give up your seat for the pregnant woman, to open the door for a lady, and to lend an arm to those needing a little extra help across the street. Those in positions of authority, success, or leadership were recognized and praised in public. These displays of honor didn't require thought. It was just the way things were.

And in the South, where Victor grew up, honor was prioritized and expected. It was mandatory for children to show respect to their elders by saying "yes, sir" or "no, ma'am." The first time I heard him address his mother this way, I was impressed. And though I loved it, I had no reference point for this code of conduct. I was raised in California, and as children, although we were expected to be unprejudiced and polite, speaking to our elders in this manner was not required. Honor was not modeled in our home.

Most of us know what it looks like when honor and respect are obviously absent in a marriage. We've all seen it. The husband may call his wife names, talk down to her, put his own needs before hers, treat her as a maid, solely seek his own pleasure, and degrade her in front of others. Conversely, I would bet we've all seen a wife who nags her husband incessantly and mocks him when she's with her girlfriends. She may look for things to complain about, make it clear she feels he is a failure, and take over his role as the leader in the home. The ugly list goes on.

A relationship absent of honor and respect is not a pretty picture. Maybe you grew up in a home like this. Sadly, I did. In my home, dishonor was taught and subsequently caught.

Needless to say, when it came to these matters in our own relationship, Victor and I faced some sizable challenges.

In karate, it is class protocol to address the instructor with a, "Yes, sir," or a "No, sir." When I took classes from Victor before we got married, as far as I was concerned, that code of honor stayed on the karate floor. It did not continue when we left the building.

And after we got married, my attitude remained unchanged.

One day, Victor and I got into a huge fight and I got physical hitting him, throwing things at him, and even kicking him. I went to my corner and he went to his. In fact, he went to spend time with his dad.

Later that day, his father came to me and in a very gentle manner said, "Eileen, it isn't right that you hit Victor."

My reaction? I thought it was absurd that I couldn't hit my own husband.

He kindly repeated himself and helped me to understand that pushing Victor's buttons in that way was both dishonoring and disrespectful.

I was honestly shocked. I had always thought it was perfectly fine for a woman to hit her husband. It was never acceptable for a husband to hit his wife of course, but I felt completely justified in hitting Victor if I chose to do so.

You may wonder how I came to this hypocritical conclusion. Believe me, the thought of this being an acceptable moral code to live by is utterly absurd to me now. As a little girl, when I heard my dad beat up my mom, all I wanted was for her to defend herself. Somehow, in my mind, I justified a woman hitting a man as a protective measure well within her rights as a wife. I told myself that was okay. However, my father-in-law's kind correction sparked a lightbulb moment for me and was the beginning of change in my heart and in our marriage.

It was obvious that my distorted definition of honor needed a serious readjustment. How could I truly honor my husband when I didn't even know what that was?

1. What is honor?

Honor is God's idea and that means it's a good one. On a very basic level, honor is giving an individual the respect he or she deserves simply because they are created in the image of God. When it comes to marriage, you cannot become one with another in body, soul, and spirit when you fail to recognize and esteem your spouse's inherent God-given value.

2. Why is honor so important?

The Bible is full of commands related to honor. We are to honor the Lord, our parents, church leaders, fellow believers, as well as those in authority. If an entire society disregards honor, it fails to value its people. When that happens, the elderly is no longer honored and respected for their hard-earned wisdom. No one gives up their seat for the pregnant woman because neither her life, nor the one she carries, are held dear. Holding a door open is merely seen as an inconvenience, and those in authority are disrespected and mocked without shame. Does any of this sound familiar? Sadly, this is where our culture is heading. Without honor, you begin to see the disintegration of individual worth, and eventually, the destruction of society. In short, we lose who we are.

3. What does honor look like in marriage?

It's easy to recognize dishonor in marriage, but sometimes we don't really stop to think about what it looks like to honor one another. Victor often shows me honor by speaking kindly of me to our children, staff, and even from the stage when he's speaking in public. He always lets me know how much he values me and wants my opinion. I honor him by listening to him, giving him my full attention when he's talking to me, letting him lead our family, and speaking respectfully to him and about him to our children. Honor can look differently to different people, so take some time to ask your husband what honor looks and feels like to him. You might be surprised.

The Bible gives us a beautiful picture of what honor looks like in marriage:

"A wife of noble character who can find. She is worth far more than rubies. Her husband has full confidence in her and lacks nothing of value. She brings him good, not harm, all the days of her life...Her husband is respected at the city gate where he takes his seat among the elders of the land...Honor her for all that her hands have done and let her works bring her praise at the city gate." Proverbs 31:10-12, 23 & 31

There is great power in honor. A wife who honors well is invaluable to her husband. It is she who, through the Lord's strength, enables and encourages her husband to be all God desires him to be.

Showing honor and respect is an outward expression of what is going on in our hearts. I mentioned earlier that dishonor was contagious in my childhood home. Resentment and bitterness accompanied the dishonor that occupied my heart. It took working with counselors and with God to get to the roots of these three things that were so prevalent in my heart and my marriage.

Today, I am able to honor and respect my husband with my whole heart. That is no small thing given our pasts, and it is the result of a long process of humbling myself, first and foremost, before God. It is a process that will continue so long as I have life on this earth, and though we still have human moments of impatience and aggravation, our marriage looks a lot different now than it did several years ago. Victor has grown into a godly man with amazing qualities. He is respected among his peers as a courageous and strong leader. God has blessed him with favor and influence in our nation and around the world. Though he is deservedly honored by many, I have come to realize that I am the most important person in his life and his honor begins, first and foremost, with me. The honor I show him through my words and actions matters more than the honor even a world leader could bestow.

Ladies, I cannot emphasize enough the importance of your role as the primary voice of encouragement in your husband's life. It is no small thing to your husband that you, as his wife, respect and honor him. Even if you question whether or not he's deserving, watch what happens when you commit to showing him honor. First, honor him as a man created in the image of God. Then ask the Lord for His vision for your husband and honor him as the man God is calling him to be.

To Think About: Is bitterness or resentment blocking your ability to show honor to your husband? What does honor look like to you? What does honor look like to your husband? What are two practical ways you can honor your husband this week?

Chapter 6
Trust

If you are not careful, what took years to build can be destroyed in minutes.

Back in California, Victor continued to struggle with PTSD while we were running a successful karate school, parenting three small children, and trying to grow in the Lord by attending church and a small group Bible study. One of the men in our group began subtly flirting with me. It was obvious to me that his intentions were not honorable. To make matters worse, he was very aware of the challenges Victor and I were facing, as Victor had confided in him. Talk about a disingenuous trust!

I was a young mom with a husband in crisis, vulnerable, and in need of encouragement. A Bible study group should have been a safe place in which to find sympathy and consolation, but I was disheartened by this friend's intentions. Thankfully, I was able to share all of this with a friend I *could* trust. My friend gave me a safe place to share my heart so that I did not have to bear this burden on my own. Not long later, we moved away, and this troubling situation resolved itself.

It seems unfathomable now, certainly after we've addressed the importance of purity and honest and open communication with your spouse, but I had to keep this man's advances a secret from my husband for more than twenty years. I didn't want to—and it was one of the hardest things I've ever done—but I knew that Victor, in his then-present state of mind, would have found and immediately killed the guy had I told him.

Thankfully, there is a happy ending to this story. After two decades and one long phone call, Victor and this man got everything out on the table. Our fellow Bible study participant took full responsibility for his actions and apologized. My justice-loving, protective husband was able to truly forgive this man. That was a miracle all in itself.

There was another time when a woman joined our ministry, claiming that God had called her to come alongside me in ministry. Within 12 months, she gave my husband an ultimatum—he had to choose between me or her. What!? Victor and I were stunned. Her departure was a given.

The very best defense to any kind of potential breach of trust is setting up your offensive plan before it happens. If it has already happened to you, your best plan is truth. We can heal from the truth but hiding it from your spouse only deepens the breach and causes greater mistrust and pain. Acknowledging the offense and getting it out into the open is the first step to take.

In our years of marriage and ministry, we've encountered many who were not to be trusted, but hidden motives and lies have a way of eventually going public. Whether it's unwanted advances, slander, or gossip, we've all endured the pain of broken trust. That's why it's so important to preserve it in our marriages at any cost.

Trust is so much more than fidelity. Trust is the full confidence that your spouse is true — true in his character, true in his words, true in his actions and most of all, true in his heart toward you, even when he makes mistakes.

One of my life verses, Proverbs 31:1, says, "The heart of her husband safely trusts her, she does him good and not evil all the days of her life." What a powerful yet vulnerable place trust has in marriage

Has trust ever been tested in your marriage? I remember a time when I really had to walk this out step by step.

When Victor started his Facebook page, he was inundated with private messages from women. This isn't uncommon for an author, speaker or ministry leader, but it can often be an area where many marriages become entangled. While Victor's intentions were to sincerely help these individuals, I was really upset.

This is when we both recognized that we needed some guidelines and wise counsel. We sought advice from a trusted couple and were able to set up the boundaries we needed to protect the well-being of our marriage and keep our trust intact.

Not one of us is above temptation and sin. Victor and I routinely ask each other if there are people, thoughts, or opportunities that could potentially get between us. I believe this is a good practice for every married couple. Trust must be preserved and maintained. Regular habits, good boundaries, and open communication are the keys to making this a reality.

The ability to trust my husband today is one of the greatest gifts I've ever been given. Victor holds my heart, and he does not take that lightly. I hold his, as well. With so many untrustworthy people in this world, the one person I need to trust most is the one God gave me to walk through life with — my beloved. It is no small thing to say that I have full confidence in who Victor is as a man of truth. I trust what he says, what he does, and most of all, his heart toward me.

To Think About: Is trusting your spouse a challenge for you? Why or why not? Has trust been broken between you? What steps can you take to breach that offense?

Chapter 7
Invisible Wounds, Visible Effects

Abuse of any kind has lasting effects on the soul. I do believe we were made to heal and to be healed completely, but the truth is that only some will live in complete freedom here on earth, while others will only experience ultimate healing in eternity.

The longer I live, the more I understand that abuse is part of our fallen world. It is the saddest reality for me to witness its lasting effects on the soul.

I see the tragic ripple effect of my husband's childhood abuse, even today. Though he has truly experienced layer after layer of healing, he still experiences the effects of the trauma as a result of his abuse, even now, decades later. We can be having an amazing time together — joking around, laughing, watching a movie or talking about something lighthearted — when he is suddenly plagued by vicious thoughts, out of nowhere. The thoughts appear with such ferocity that it's hard to stop them. They are intrusive and usually accusatory. Sadly, with all the lies he believed as a child, among them was the belief that he wasn't—and never would be--good enough. Even today, as a man of God who has been and continues to be used by the Lord in amazing, powerful and life-changing ways, you would think he would be immune to those kinds of thoughts. The enemy of our souls is relentless!

It is in those times of great fatigue and exhaustion that the enemy takes advantage of our human weaknesses.

1 Peter 5:8 says, "Be alert and of sober mind. Your enemy, the devil, prowls around like a roaring lion looking for someone to devour." Wounded places of the soul are, in the eyes of the wicked one, some of the best and easiest ones to attack. Make no mistake, his aim is to eventually devour us whole.

So, what is the antidote? How do we overcome lies from the enemy? How do we help our spouse do the same? Here's what Victor and I do. When my husband is attacked by the enemy's lies, we ask God to help ease his mind, asking Him to speak truth to the overwhelming thoughts. When Victor hears truth, it helps his mind to respond and his soul to calm down. I often put on praise music and Bible teachings that speak and reaffirm the truth. Then, I pray over his mind and against any and every force coming against him and against our marriage. I plead the precious blood of Jesus over him from the crown of his head to the bottom of his feet. I do this whenever the need arises.

And though these times can be challenging, God uses them to grow my compassion toward my husband and toward other married couples who are dealing with the effects of trauma. It has also grown my compassion for those who have endured the horrors of abuse — physical, mental, and sexual. Walking through this healing journey with my Victor has shown me that God is truly able to restore and heal a broken soul.

Victor and I have faced and overcome so many challenges together. We understand just how difficult marriage can be, which is why we make a habit of reaching out to other couples who are struggling. Doing so undoubtedly makes us a target of the enemy, but as we come alongside others to battle these hardships, we have come to find that God is on our side and will always give us the victory when we cling to Him and stand on His Word.

But even in a marriage grounded in the Lord, the ripple effects of abuse can be overwhelming and can cause second-hand trauma to those closest to the abused. Second-hand trauma is lesser known and often overlooked, as attention is directed to the acute symptoms or hemorrhaging of the family member who actually has PTSD. Second-hand trauma can be even more dangerous than PTSD, simply because it goes unrecognized and is seemingly much harder to validate.

And yet, that is exactly what is needed most.

Second-hand trauma often produces feelings of anger, resentment, and bitterness. We watched our older children struggle with these feelings as a result of witnessing their father struggle with PTSD. They also saw me react in anger and heard the ugly things I said to their dad. How could they not be affected by their parents' behavior?

So how is a spouse to deal with the anger he or she feels? How does a child cope when they lack the ability to control their circumstances? How do they deal with the resentment they harbor toward their abused loved one—one who is now, intentionally or not, the cause of such chaos and turmoil within the home? This is why I strongly believe that those who suffer from second-hand trauma need help, too.

Recognizing that second-hand trauma is real is the first step. Children and spouses need to be validated for the pain and trauma they are experiencing, as well as the situations they face that are beyond their control. Finding a trauma specialist is a good place to start the process of healing. These professionals are well aware of the devastating, far-reaching effects of abuse, as well as the challenges of living with someone who has PTSD.

I was always concerned about telling anyone what was happening in our home. My husband was in ministry; what would they think? Thankfully I was able to confide in my mom, my twin sister, and a close girlfriend. The burden was too great to carry alone.

And here's the interesting thing: after Victor experienced so much healing, it was then that *my* anger, bitterness, and resentment started to surface. I couldn't hide my feelings anymore. I found a woman who works with wives of men in ministry, and she not only understood the pressures of ministry life but related to the secrets many hide because of the unique challenges and circumstances they face. She helped me deal with the destructive emotions I was feeling, and she helped me get to the root of my anger and bitterness. This was truly life-changing for me. A ton of baggage was lifted from my soul and my heart was freed from the hidden, toxic emotions I had lived with ever since I was a little girl.

Another ripple effect of abuse that often goes unnoticed is self-sabotage. I've seen this behavior in people close to me and in others I've known throughout my life. Self-sabotage operates like a safety valve in those who have experienced trauma. When circumstances are out of their control or they find themselves in a situation where things are *too* normal or *too* quiet, they become uncomfortable and are unable to accept what is ordinary to others. It is sad to think that peace and calm can be *that* foreign to them.

I've seen people purposefully create chaos in order to feel in control of their surroundings. I've witnessed others destroy relationships for no apparent reason. I believe they are so used to instability and dysfunction that normalcy often scares them.

In our travels around the country, Victor and I have heard heartbreaking stories where this seems to be the case. Many involve a spouse who, out of the blue, up and leaves their whole family without an explanation. When this happens, the unfortunate common denominator is often some kind of abuse.

Abuse affects the soul, our innermost being. The enemy of our souls has three purposes in any person's life: to steal, to kill, and to destroy. John 10:10 makes that clear, "The thief comes only to steal and kill and destroy; I have come that they may have life and have it to the full."

If our enemy can't kill a person, he will try to steal what God has prepared for him or her. In marriage, he comes to steal a couple's joy, peace, trust, and commitment, and can even rob them of a whole lifetime together. If he can't do that, he will try to destroy them. I know many in the church, including ministry leaders, whose families, ministries or reputations have been utterly destroyed. The enemy of our soul is relentless!

But our God is more powerful than the enemy, and He is in the business of redemption. This is what keeps Victor and I speaking out against the wicked one, coming alongside couples to help them see how the enemy is working against them in their marriage.

For my own marriage, I pray against the ways in which the enemy tries to steal what God has planned for us. I pray for our children, who have been impacted by second-hand trauma. Victor shares publicly and has proven time and time again that "our past does not determine our future, nor does it define us." Victor is an incredible man of God and I believe it is because of his experiences that he is able to touch thousands of people, young and old, who have suffered all kinds of trauma, and offer them real hope. He is living proof that they can overcome anything and become all that God created them to be.

I'm so thankful that through all of our family struggles our children have been able to process their thoughts, fears, and emotions with trained counselors who have and continue to help them heal and grow in healthy ways. It makes me smile to think we now have three grown children who are each married to a godly spouse. They did not bring into their marriages anywhere near the amount of baggage we did. They may have brought some, but it was more the size of a carry-on instead of a checked bag.

We often talk about the fact that someday, when we are older, the enemy's attacks will be old news. Until then, we continue to battle unseen forces and their relentless attacks. We continue to speak and reaffirm truth, and to walk in each victory. Even though we know who wins the war, the battles we face here on earth are still very real and have very real power, but they cannot overpower God, His Truth, or the precious blood of Jesus.

In marriage, issues like abuse are some of the hardest to work through with your spouse. But God can use you as an instrument of His love, to be His hands, heart, and voice, and play a crucial role in your spouse's healing. Wouldn't that make all the difficulties, challenges, and hardships you've endured worth it? Or maybe you have been the victim of abuse and are in need of God's care and healing. For both roles, Victor and I know the road can be long and hard.

Life will not always feel this intense. If you cling to God and allow Him to take your pressures, pain, and sorrows, He will give you a supernatural understanding and peace that He will work all things together for your good. The very name of our ministry is All Things Are Possible...because with God, they are.

Don't ever give up, God can redeem your past!

To Think About: If abuse has impacted you or your spouse, how have you felt its ripple effects in your marriage? What lie has the enemy told your spouse over and over? What lie does he continue to tell you? Think about two practical ways you and your spouse can help each other combat lies with the truth.

Chapter 8
When It's Time to Go

Like most brides, I came into my marriage with a heart full of love and excitement. I didn't know the road ahead, but I loved my husband and I knew he loved me.

Just a year after we said, "I do," we had our first child, and our second came a short seventeen months later. We were young and open to whatever adventures God had in store for us. Life was very full and very good.

Not long after our third baby was born, Victor severed his right hamstring during a karate belt test. His physical injury, as well as the pressure to provide for our family and keep our business running, weighed constantly and heavily on his mind. Depression set in. These overwhelming factors came together to create the perfect storm. And the thing about storms is that though they can be powerful and destructive, they can also be cleansing. God was allowing this one for such a purpose.

All the emotional pain and trauma that lay dormant in Victor's soul began to surface. As Victor says, he was no longer able to "keep the beach ball underwater." Eventually, the pressure forced it to pop up, causing sudden and real damage.

This is a perfect picture of what happened to Victor and to our small, growing family.

At the time, though, I had no idea what was going on, or more importantly, why. Victor started to behave in a manner many would call irrational and erratic, and even bizarre. As his instability increased, I became more and more overwhelmed. The thought of separating was scary and uncertain. It wasn't what I wanted—at all—but I knew something had to change.

But was it the right thing to do? As a Christian wife, I wondered about whether it was okay to separate from my husband, just as he was starting to unravel. Honestly, I didn't know what to do. My heart was conflicted with anger and compassion. I didn't want this homelife for our children, but I loved my husband and didn't want him to suffer alone.

Having experienced an unstable childhood, I knew I could not expose our children to the potential fear and trauma Victor's behavior could cause. My mom knew it, too, and encouraged me to bring our children to her house.

When I found the horrible words, Victor had written on our bathroom wall, and the dagger he had stuck in another wall, I knew it was time to take her up on the offer. Victor and I actually made the decision together. He agreed that it wasn't good for the children to live in the midst of this craziness. He loaded up our van and sent me, our two toddlers, and our baby away.

This was hands down one of the most painful moments of our marriage...for both of us. But as He so often does, God used His Word and the people He brought into our lives to help and encourage us.

During that time, I clung to a verse familiar to many: *Trust in the Lord with all your heart and lean not on your own understanding. In all your ways acknowledge Him and He shall direct your paths* (Proverbs 3:5-6).

Years earlier, when I was single and working in a physical therapy clinic, the daughter of one of our patients created a beautiful drawing for me and put this very Scripture on it. My boss looked at her artwork and offered to reduce the size so that I could carry it with me. I'm so glad he did. I carried her artwork in my wallet and memorized this verse. I had no idea just how much it would anchor me in the storms that were yet to come.

We stayed at my mom's house for about a week, and then Victor came to bring us back home. I was struck by how different he seemed—so broken. He was still suffering, but he was taking medication to help control the episodes of angry, violent behavior. Even so, I knew he needed additional help. I wanted him to be better for all of us. So, we came back home together.

What do you do when your spouse behaves in ways you know are wrong or even dangerous? I don't believe there is a universal answer here, as there can be many underlying reasons for such behavior, and many appropriate responses. Looking back, had I known that Victor was acting like this because he was suffering from PTSD, I would have found specialized help, and much, much sooner.

PTSD can manifest in many different symptoms, wreaking havoc on a marriage, a family, a business, or a friendship. Sadly, and far too often, it can even convince the one suffering to take his or her own life. Those suffering often feel suicide is the only way to end their pain, and the only way to not burden their loved ones. If you notice a loved one acting out, consider whether or not they could be affected by PTSD, especially if there was any type of trauma in their past.

Understand that PTSD affects the entire person. If you suspect your spouse is dealing with it, please don't wait for something devastating to happen. It needs immediate attention. There is good information and many forms of treatment available today. Do your homework and commit to walk through this process together.

If you have children in the home, be aware that second-hand trauma is very real and valid and can cause equally devastating effects. Considering such, be aware of what kinds of unhealthy behavior you allow your children to be exposed to. Do not be afraid to take action when needed.

Additionally, the church needs to understand that trauma affects the human soul. People who are dealing with trauma often self-medicate with drugs, alcohol, adultery, and pornography. As I mentioned, some even commit suicide to escape it. Accepting Jesus Christ as his or her Lord and Savior doesn't exempt God's children from trauma. Offering suggestions to read God's Word or pray more as a solution to find healing are not only misguided, but ill-informed. The sad reality is that people who suffer from PTSD often have a difficult time doing either of those things. Some are on medication to help manage their anxiety, panic attacks, and fear. Many live in a constant state of insomnia, which makes it nearly impossible to focus on anything. Others have begged God to help them and yet they haven't experienced relief. These suffering souls need trained professionals who acknowledge that God is able to bring healing to the soul to walk with them through their trauma.

This process cannot begin, though, if denial is encouraged in any way. Our ministry has produced two films, *Triggered* and *Triggered Too,* to shed light on this important subject. To date, tens of thousands have seen these films, and many have responded by sharing their own struggles with PTSD with us.

Whether it's PTSD or an equally challenging issue that's impacting your marriage, the decision to leave is never an easy one.

I can't tell you when it's time to leave, but I can tell you that your marriage is—or should be—one of the safest places to go through this very challenging season of life. If it's not a safe place, then it's wise to remove yourself from the situation until it is. No problem can be tackled by the two of you when one of you is in danger.

I have spoken with women who found themselves in a situation where their spouse is in a pattern of cheating and lying—a constant cycle of apologies without permanent change. This is another situation where a separation may be appropriate. Again, if one spouse is causing harm, I believe the other can and should draw a line in the sand. The ultimate purpose of a separation is to demand action for healthy change in your spouse and in your marriage.

When we say, "I do," I don't believe we really know what we're committing to on that day. How could we? This is a solemn vow you make throughout your life, not just when everything is good or easy. If separation is the right choice, then you need to make sure your heart is in the right place. Be certain you are doing it for the right reasons. If you are just fed up with your spouse or your expectations are not being met, the issue may not solely fall on your spouse. You may play a role in it as well. Before making the decision to separate, take time to evaluate your heart and see if it is lined up with God's heart for you and your marriage. There is not a marriage out there that has not or will not go through hard and challenging times. God created marriage to last a lifetime, and in a lifetime, you will have all kinds of challenges.

Don't settle for a broken marriage. Look at how God created marriage to be and how He wants men, who are made in His image, to live and love their wives. Look at how He wants women, who are also made in His image, to help, complete, love, and respect their husbands. When we love and respect each other, we don't allow ungodly behavior to continue week after week, month after month, and year after year. Allowing Victor to continue down the destructive path he was on would not have been good for him, and it most certainly would not have been good for our marriage and children. I'm so grateful that God led us down a path of healing. If I'm honest, we're still on it today. It's a process. Life happens, and even though Victor has been healed from many past issues, we still have life to live.

While our challenges have been many and often overwhelming, I can honestly say that I would not change our past. Our love and commitment is so much deeper today. We truly know each other. One look into each other's eyes speaks volumes and is a language only the two of us can understand. We have walked through fire and did not get burned. We are together and we are one.

To Think About: If you are considering a separation, is there a godly person in your life on whom you can rely for counsel? If you aren't in this position, can you think of someone who is that might need your prayer and encouragement right now?

Chapter 9
Temptation

Temptation comes in many forms. Some obvious, others less so. In our years of ministry, we've seen some pretty bizarre and brazen attempts to break up our marriage.

It should come as no surprise, given the sex-saturated culture we live in, that the enemy is crafty, and he is dedicated to destroying marriages. His traps can be bold, but they can also be subtle and seemingly innocent. We cannot allow room for even a sliver of compromise. The Bible gives great advice in I Thessalonians 5:22, "Abstain from all appearance of evil." We try to apply this verse, even in the little things.

For example, when Victor speaks, many ask to take pictures afterwards. When I'm present, we don't let anyone stand in between us when photos are taken. We always have the person stand on either side of us, never in the middle. It may seem like a small thing, but we've found that the small things are where the enemy often gains the largest foothold.

We've gained wisdom over the years and learned a few truths that have helped us to better deal with the temptation that inevitably comes, in some form or another.

First, we openly admit that we are not immune to sexual temptation. No one is. We are both human, made of flesh and blood. We are both sinners. As wives, we have to get over any humiliation or disappointment we may feel when our spouse struggles with this issue. Our husbands are human. They're not immune to temptation and neither are we.

Victor and I have both had dangerous thoughts, weaknesses, and temptations—especially when we're at odds with one another. Our very weaknesses are often the areas where we are most susceptible to temptation. For me, the lack of kindness I received from my father created a void—a longing in my heart for kindness from others. Many of you may be able to relate. Temptation often arises in our most tender places; the enemy may target them in his attempts to dismantle your marriage. Acknowledging and understanding our weaknesses together is a huge step toward guarding our hearts so that we do not fall prey to temptations when they arise. I have been blessed with a loving, kindhearted husband who has helped to strengthen, grow, and mature the weak and wounded places of my heart.

Second, we must recognize the tremendous power we have as one. When we are united as husband and wife under the lordship of Christ, we can not only win our battles with `temptation, but we will come out of them stronger, together. The tactics of the wicked one are deliberate, strategic, and ruthless, but God has the upper hand. He masterfully designed marriage to overcome the enemy's challenges. With God on our side, we can and will be victorious.

Third, I make sure my husband knows he is loved and safe with me. When Victor is traveling, I know all too well the temptations that the enemy would love for him to fall into. To have a man of God give in to sexual temptation is not only a notch in the enemy's belt, but a disgrace to the God we speak of, His character, and His intended purpose for us as man and wife. Knowing full well this will be a strategy Satan employs while my beloved is away from me, I shore up my husband's heart and soul by making sure that before he travels, his cup is full of my love. I want him to be full and satisfied, with no part of him left hungry or wanting. My husband knows he is loved, wanted, and that his wife is waiting at home for him when he returns. If he's tempted while we're apart, he knows he can call me and that I will pray for and with him. We will dismantle the attacks from the wicked one together. I am forever on his side and one of his greatest allies.

We have found that it is helpful to form a battle plan together, so that you are prepared to fight as one when you face temptation. Here are some of the practical ways Victor and I fight together:

1. We are honest about temptation. Victor occasionally shares his thoughts about this in social media posts, and I'm so glad he does. I believe his honesty can help those who silently struggle. There is no shame in being tempted and avoiding the issue will not make it go away.

2. We talk to each other when we are tempted. When we are tempted by the enemy, we tell each other. My husband often receives full-on, open invitations from women, especially when he travels. He tells me and I don't hold it against him. I know what he's up against. I pray for and with him and he does the same for me. I am on his side and he is on mine. We regularly check in on each other, asking, "How are you doing? Are you getting any weird thoughts? Is anyone trying to gain your attention or affection?" This level of vulnerability and honesty unites us, making it that much harder for the enemy to divide and conquer. Wives never forget that you are your husband's strongest ally in this fight.

3. We do not have secrets. The enemy does his best work in the dark. Keeping secrets from your spouse invites him in and asks him to get to work! There is no need for private conversations with members of the opposite sex, and never any reason to have secret accounts. We give each other our passwords and login information—for our phones as well as all of our social media accounts.

4. We keep the inner circle closed. One of the best things about marriage is the intimate bond that exists just between the two of you. Safeguard that. Don't let anyone else in; there must be a place in your marriage that exists only for the two of you. One is the marriage bed, which should be a guarded place of sacredness. The other is the sacred realm of the heart, which involves complete vulnerability, transparency, and trust between you and your spouse. I don't believe other people should know your spouse to the same extent that you do. While I share some very personal things with my twin sister, I will never share the realm of my heart that belongs only to my husband. Keeping these things set apart for your marriage is essential to having a healthy one.

5. We forgive often. The enemy is always looking for that opportunity to get a foot in the door and he knows that unforgiveness gives him that perfect opportunity. Ephesians 4:26-27 shows us; Be angry, and do not sin do not let the sun go down on your wrath, nor give place to the devil. IF we go to sleep with anger in our heart towards one another we are in sin and have given a place for the devil. We may dismiss our feelings of being offended and maybe just stuff them down into our hearts, but the devil won't, and will use it against us as we harbor those until they become toxic behaviors causing bitterness and resentment. Jesus warns us that if we do not forgive those who trespass against us, He won't forgive our trespasses. Matthew 6:14

Though we have healthy habits and boundaries in place, temptation doesn't always come in the form of a bold offer. It is often far more subtle and over the past decade, social media has certainly altered the playing field. We now have instant access to millions of people—friends, acquaintances and total strangers alike. Private conversations with anyone you want to talk to are only a few keystrokes away. Breaking a vow can be as simple as typing a name into your search bar and initiating a conversation.

Social media has destroyed more relationships and marriages than we'd care to admit. Several years ago, while Victor was traveling, we got a taste for how the enemy can use this tool to drive couples apart.

Before Victor left, things were completely fine between the two of us. He was speaking at a church, and during his trip, I decided to check social media. I saw people responding positively to the message Victor had given that Sunday. Many commented about how and why his message had blessed them. This is not unusual; he usually receives lots of glowing feedback after he speaks! This time, however, I honed-in on one specific woman who went on and on about how much she loved Victor, how she thought he was amazing, and blah, blah, blah.

Something in me snapped.

Over the years, I've grown accustomed to people pouring out adulation over my husband, but this time it just didn't sit well. I wondered if these women would appreciate seeing glowing comments from other women on *their* husband's social media page.

When Victor is away, I am usually very aware of the ways the wicked one tries to tempt *him*, attacking his mind and spirit. During his trips, the enemy is also busy causing problems for us at home, which usually manifest in increased fighting and division between my children. I was so accustomed to looking out for the normal plans of attack that this attempt really caught me off guard.

It never occurred to me that this might be a deliberate set-up. It never occurred to me that he would attack *me* in this way.

When I asked Victor, what was going on with this specific woman, he said, "It's nothing. It's not that big of a deal."

Wrong answer. It was a big deal to me, and in my mind, he had just dismissed my thoughts and concerns, which in turn made me even more angry. For the next two days, I obsessively read this woman's comments, rehearsing the situation over and over in my mind.

Without thinking clearly, I gave into my emotions. Hook, line, and sinker.

Anger welled up in my heart. I wanted my husband to feel what I was feeling. I wanted him to see how it felt to have others pour the same adulation over me. How would he feel if men were talking this way about me?

I wanted revenge. So, what did I do? I logged into Facebook and looked up an old high school boyfriend. I wrote him a private, brief message. He wrote me back. Victor returned from his trip, got on Facebook and saw the conversation. He was absolutely sick to his stomach.

When he asked me about it, it angered me that he would even have the gall to question me, after dismissing my similar feelings. He was feeling what I had, and he didn't like it any more than I did. This was exactly what I wanted. Revenge. Blinded by anger, I thought my actions were completely justified. After all, I wasn't trying to start anything with this old boyfriend, I just wanted Victor to understand how much it hurt me to have women reach out to him on social media.

This experience was a wake-up call for both of us.

We confided in a couple who was also in full-time ministry. They gave us godly advice to help us better navigate this challenge. We started by making some practical changes. First, Victor disabled the private message feature and made it known that he would not answer private messages. Second, I deleted my personal Facebook account and we made Victor's ministry account our shared account. Third, we drew clearer boundaries in our ministry procedures. Victor didn't have to change who he was, but he did have to change the perception that he was available to talk to anyone and everyone with a need. Staff members now respond to the needs of individuals who reach out to our ministry. These simple changes have helped us make social media work *for* our marriage, not *against* it.

We look back now and see the potential damage this could have done to our marriage. We've seen several marriages fall prey to the snare of social media, resulting in adultery, and ultimately divorce. It's a dangerous trap, one that works all too often.

I believe that in time, social media will be seen as another fad that has come and gone. Like a new, shiny car, it too will rust and be discarded. Our social media "friends" that we gave so much time and credence to will not be around in 20 years. Marriage, however, is a commitment intended to endure the test of time. We must honor it and one another in such a way that it will.

Two verses come to mind when I think of temptation.

I Peter 5:8 "Be alert and of sober mind. Your enemy the devil prowls around like a roaring lion, seeking whom he may devour."

Ephesians 4:27 "Be angry and do not sin, do not let the sun go down on your wrath, nor give place to the devil."

The enemy is looking for a way in—any way in—to devour you and your marriage. Do not give him the opportunity to succeed. No matter how small or innocent some interactions may seem, I encourage you to be honest with your spouse when you are tempted, to set boundaries and fight together. The enemy is no match for God's power in and through the two of you.

To Think About: Is temptation something you can openly talk about with your spouse? Why or why not? Consider talking about healthy boundaries you can set in order to fight temptation together?

Chapter 10
The Bottom Fell Out

Shortly after starting our ministry, we realized that our largest audience of hurting, incarcerated juveniles was in Texas. Eager to serve them well, we moved our young family—now with four little ones—from our home in Colorado to Texas. Life was tough in Texas. It felt as if we went straight from the frying pan into the fire.

Our time there began with heartbreak. The very day we moved into our brand-new home; I miscarried our fifth baby. I had gone to my doctor earlier that month, excited to have an ultrasound and to confirm the date of our little one's arrival. Instead of hearing a heartbeat, we heard the devastating news that our baby was no longer living. While we knew this precious one was already in heaven, our hearts were broken. We prayed and decided to let my body miscarry naturally, as God created it to do. We were both emotionally raw but worked through our grief together. I had heard a song the Sunday before we moved that brought comfort to my heart: *Blessed be the name of the Lord, blessed be Your name…You give and take away, my heart will choose to say, Lord, blessed be Your name.*

I still think of our little one whenever I hear that song and know we will see him or her in heaven one day.

We held onto that hope and pressed on.

In 2003, we officially launched our ministry to reach incarcerated youth, naming it *All Things Possible,* because with God, miracles are truly possible today. Victor began sharing his testimony, using martial arts as the platform in dozens of prison facilities all over the state. Texas, at the time, had the largest population of juvenile offenders in the country. He was working 14- to 16-hour days and our ministry grew steadily to include more staff members so that we could meet the requests for help that were pouring in.

One year after we miscarried, I gave birth to our sixth baby, whom we affectionately refer to as our caboose. Born just 10 days after Victor turned 40, he was just as God told Victor he would be—a son. He was the sweetest gift to our family, and with this little one, I knew our quiver was full.

Our family and our ministry were growing, but so was an intense resistance.

We reluctantly sent our three older children to the public junior high and high schools. Looking back, this was one of the worst decisions we could have made. Our children, who previously homeschooled or attended private schools, were now in the mouth of the lion's den. We made this decision because of the opportunities public school offered. We naively believed that because we were Christians, God's grace would allow us to bypass all of the perversion and ungodly behavior in the public-school system.

We were so very wrong.

Within six weeks of starting school, our children began asking us why we believed homosexuality was wrong, and about specific, sexual terminology they were overhearing in the hallways at school. Divorced families were rampant in this community and morality was nowhere to be found. This was foreign territory to our children, and they were not equipped with the needed tools to navigate the situations and issues they now regularly faced. To make matters worse, one of our teenagers was in full-on rebellion mode.

In the moment, it felt as if the gates of hell had opened up to destroy our family and our ministry.

Do you know that we are constantly fighting a spiritual battle? Though we read about it in Scripture, and at times sense its reality, we often go through our daily lives unaware of how or what the enemy is doing. We learned the hard way that he is very methodical and strategic. And while we knew many verses about warfare, we had no idea how to engage in the battle.

We were about to learn.

Victor's first lesson in this is one we will never forget. He was speaking at a maximum-security youth facility where the girls sat on one side of the gymnasium and the boys on the other. As Victor began to share the Gospel, one girl started savagely clawing at her neck right where she sat in the bleachers. The girls around her moved away. The guards did, too, and pleaded with Victor to help her. Victor thought to himself, "You're the guards. You help her!" The guards in this girl's unit already knew she had inexplicable, strange powers.

At the conclusion of his talk, after the youth were dismissed, Victor went to visit this girl in her cell. While he was talking, she began to manifest again. Her eyes closed and Victor saw reptile scales on her eyelids. A voice that was not hers spoke. "You disgust me," it said to Victor. It then went on to tell him specific things about his life that no one else could have known. The voice said, "I will destroy your marriage, your finances, and your daughter." Victor knew it was a demon.

He asked the young woman, "Do you want to be free from this?" In her own voice, she said, "If I do, will you Christians forget about me? Cause I know he won't," referring to Satan.

Victor went back the next day and this young woman, who was dedicated to the devil as a baby by her Satanist father, prayed to receive Jesus! Isn't that amazing?

From that day on, the resistance we faced only increased.

Strange things began to happen. I could feel a profoundly evil presence in our home; mocking and rebellious spirits had clearly made their way in. The spiritual environment of the town we were living in did not help either. It became obvious that perversity and darkened, reprobate minds were rampant. The oppression was overwhelming. I had never struggled with depression, but out of left field, a dark period of depression engulfed my being. The enemy's hand was responsible, and I felt as though our whole family was falling apart.

We were in the ring with no gloves on to fight.

We called our pastor back in Colorado to ask for help and he suggested we meet with a man he knew who understood the demonic realm. This man prayed for us and taught us how this realm operates, equipping us to stand in our God-given authority as His children.

Looking back, we realize we were participants in a condensed training course that could have been named, "How to battle in the unseen realm." God gave us the faith we needed to exercise our authority over the demonic realm, and to eventually teach others how to do the same.

As we grew in our understanding and authority, we began praying for people harassed and tormented by demons. God showed Victor that many of their struggles, addictions, and relationship issues resulted from demonic assignments on their lives. Once an assignment had been revealed, lies were exposed and freedom came. Sometimes, demons have a "right" to stay, simply because an individual has given them permission to be there. If that is the case, demons will not relinquish their ground until the sin is dealt with. It may be something seemingly small, such as bitterness or unforgiveness, but Hebrews 12:15 says, "See to it that no one falls short of the grace of God and that no bitter root grows up to cause trouble and defile many." That bitter root can cause tremendous damage if it is not dealt with. It can be something unassuming and quiet like resentment or unbridled anger. In either case, an individual must deal with these areas of sin in order to remove the ground the enemy holds.

Unfortunately, some believers struggle with this approach. We are occasionally asked if this method really works. In the many years we've been doing this, the answer has come in seeing hundreds of people set free from cycles of addiction, destructive relationships, and tormenting lies.

We won the battle against demonic spirits in our home, but the battle continued on other fronts.

Victor's PTSD resurfaced and he began to unravel again. Unfortunately, PTSD does not just go away. Many things, including stress, can cause it to resurface. Getting help is not admitting a weakness, nor does it mean you are any less of a person. It means you are strong and that you understand your soul needs attention. We found our family in a place where each one of our souls needed attention, and we knew we needed to spend the time, resources, and energy necessary to make that happen.

Texas now held very challenging memories and it became obvious we needed time, space, and most of all, healing. We decided it was time to head back to California.

Over the next seven years that we spent in California, we saw healing and growth in each one of our children. Our older children graduated from high school, went on to Bible college and got jobs. During that time, we decided to put Victor's life story in print, publishing his autobiography, *The Victor Marx Story: With God, All Things are Possible.* We also decided to tell his story in a film, "The Victor Marx Story: When Impossible is the Only Way Out," so that Victor could virtually "visit" every youth facility in the nation with a message of hope in Jesus Christ. The day the movie premiered; we rented a big movie theater in Temecula. Two theaters sold out and we had to open up two more showings that night. The film even outsold "The Hunger Games"!

We were so excited for the potential number of lives that would be changed by this film. However, we did not anticipate the effects of the overwhelming response.

Everywhere we went, people now recognized Victor. From Costco to ballet recitals to quiet romantic getaways. Many could relate to his story and when they saw him, they wanted to share their own. We would be out on a date and people would stop and want to talk to him. Most of the time they didn't even notice we were on a date! We had people leaving notes on our door...and we lived in a gated community. The loss of privacy was overwhelming. So much so that in time, we felt it was time to leave.

We put our house on the market, sold it within 90 days, put our things in storage, packed up our two younger children in our motorhome and headed out to find a new home. We had three states in mind — Oregon, Montana and Colorado — all of which would provide more privacy than we were getting at the time. Our good friends lived in a part of Colorado that appealed to us and we thought that if we could live close to them, we would move there in a heartbeat. Lo and behold, we discovered that one of their neighbors might be interested in selling her home, though she wasn't ready to do so just yet. We saw it, loved it, and roughly 30 days later, moved into a home right next to our good friends and in a state we loved. God had gone before us, meeting our needs and even our wants.

These were some of the toughest years in our marriage, but we learned how to fight against the enemy—together. We learned how to war for our marriage, for our children, and for those God called us to serve. It was exhausting and overwhelming, but Jesus proved there is a love so deep that it's worth fighting and dying for. It is that love that gives us a reason and a purpose to live. It is that love that helps us overcome. In marriage. In ministry. In everything.

That love is more than worth the fight.

To Think About: Can you think of a time when you felt like you were dealing with a force that was bringing havoc and chaos into your life and marriage? Could it be that it was from the demonic realm? Take time to discuss these times and situations. Pray and ask the Holy Spirit to help you identify the truth about these.

Chapter 11
Victorious Spiritual Warfare

The institution of marriage is under great attack, and those who are rescuing people from hell are high-value targets. We must understand that the enemy of our souls is not only working against us, but more than anything, he wants for us as husbands and wives to work against one another.

Let's face it. The wrecking of a Christian marriage can destroy the image of Christ and His church, leaving many with a bad taste in their mouth not only toward marriage, but toward Christ as well.

Marriage is a mysterious union designed to stand the test of time. It mirrors the supernatural relationship between Jesus and His bride, the Church. Jesus loves His bride, so much so that He came to serve and die for her. In so doing, he modeled how a husband is to love his wife. The Church responds to the selfless love of Jesus in submission, respect, and honor. We, as wives, are called to do the same. It takes a lifetime to both understand and live out this mysterious, sacrificial union. It is the Holy Spirit at the center of this union who enables a husband to die and a wife to submit. Together, the two are one. Satan hates that marriage is the fingerprint of God on the earth, and relentlessly works to demolish it any way he can.

Which is where spiritual warfare comes in. So, what exactly is spiritual warfare?

You've likely heard the term and maybe even heard differing definitions, but let's look at how the war got started. In Ezekiel 28:14-18, God describes the beginning of this war with Satan who, at one time, held a high position in the angelic realm:

"You were anointed as a guardian cherub, for so I ordained you. You were on the holy mount of God; you walked among the fiery stones. You were blameless in your ways from the day you were created till wickedness was found in you. Through your widespread trade you were filled with violence and you sinned. So, I drove you in disgrace from the mount of God, and I expelled you, guardian cherub, from among the fiery stones. Your heart became proud on account of your beauty, and you corrupted your wisdom because of your splendor. So, I threw you to the earth; I made a spectacle of you before kings. By your many sins and dishonest trade, you have desecrated your sanctuaries. So, I made a fire come out from you, and it consumed you, and I reduced you to ashes on the ground in the sight of all who were watching."

The war between God and Satan continues to this day and will end on the appointed day, as God sees fit. It manifests in invisible and visible attacks on God's people, which is what we commonly refer to as "spiritual warfare."

When Satan was cast down to earth, Scripture tells us that a third of all the angels went with him. We refer to these fallen angels as demons, spirit beings who have no physical bodies but are able to move to and fro across the earth. They can influence human beings with thoughts of any kind, including accusations and temptations. They are able to cause, though they are not always the cause, of financial struggles, relationship problems, physical ailments, and even death. Their goal is to steal, kill, and destroy as many human souls as they can through the havoc they wreak.

Most of us have experienced their attacks, whether or not we realized from whence they came. How can we recognize spiritual warfare in our lives and in our marriages?

Over our years of ministry, Victor and I have become more aware of how the enemy works, which enables us to effectively fight against him. He starts with us as individuals, whispering lies in our ears. For example, have you ever looked in the mirror and heard, *you are ugly,* or *You are fat,* or *Nobody likes you?* Think about it. Are you hearing the words, "You are" or are you hearing the words, "I am"? If someone is speaking to you, then you are hearing a toxic whisper from an unseen, but very real world. It is a deliberate, strategic plan to get you to see yourself negatively, that you might be weakened and destroyed over time.

We will all face challenging circumstances in life—things we may never fully understand while on this earth. It is often hard to discern whether our circumstances are caused by the enemy or whether he is opportunistically using them to his advantage. Scripture tells us in 2 Corinthians 2:11 not to be ignorant regarding the Devil's strategies in our lives. Here are some questions to ask yourself to help you determine if the enemy may be at work:

• Are any of these circumstances being caused by my own choices?

• Am I believing a lie about myself that may perpetuate these circumstances?

• Is there a vow or agreement I've made that runs counter to what God has said about me in His Word? If so, is this giving the enemy permission to operate in my life?

If you answered "yes" to any of these questions, you can overcome every lie in Jesus' name! You can do this by inviting His powerful presence into this area of your life. Next, acknowledge the lies you've been believing, which are anything contrary to the Word of God, and confess that they are just that — lies. Ask the Holy Spirit to set you free from patterns of thinking that hold you captive. Ask Him to cleanse and renew this part of your mind and soul and to show you the truth. Then, begin speaking truth over yourself, your circumstances, your marriage, your children, and family. Know that can be a process that takes time, but Scripture does promise us in John 8:32 that "the truth will set you free." You are made to overcome, and God will help you do just that!

Other ways the enemy can and does attack individuals are described clearly in the book of Job. Satan actually asks God to remove His hedge of protection from Job in order to prove that the only reason Job serves God is because of his wealth and prosperity. God removed his protection, allowing Satan to physically afflict Job and to also kill all of his children and livestock. God allowed Job to be tested and his faith to be proven.

I believe the same happens to us today. Oftentimes physical ailments and sicknesses test us and show us what's going on in our hearts. Other times we're tested by the consequences of our own choices. We won't always understand the why's here on earth, but if we are walking with God and are experiencing hard trials of any kind, I think we can always ask God to show us if it's the enemy working to gain a foothold in our lives.

Those are few ways the enemy attacks us as individuals and gains ground, but how do we recognize his tactics when it comes to marriage?

One of the most obvious—and prevalent—forms of spiritual attacks on marriage is pornography. This has to be a favorite tool of the enemy. He uses this to prey upon human wounds and weaknesses to ultimately destroy everyone involved. He is ruthless. How many men (and women) today are caught in pornography's vicious cycle? How many have lost everything because of it?

We know the enemy comes to steal, kill, and destroy, and that pattern is key to recognizing spiritual attacks in your marriage. Let's take a look at how the enemy does this, using pornography as an example:

• Stage #1: STEAL

Pornography is a readily available weapon capable of destroying marriages. It is such a powerful weapon because it is most often viewed in private and kept a secret. The enemy encourages this secrecy with shame. *What would your wife think of you if she knew what you were doing? What a failure you are. It's best not to tell her anyway.* He then works against the wife, building up suspicion and increasing her insecurity. *You must not be enough. If only you were more attractive, then maybe he wouldn't be drawn to this. You can't trust him. He'll always lie to you.* Wives, when we allow these whispers to take hold of us, they develop roots. These roots cause bitterness and resentment. These feelings will impede any natural desire for sexual relations with your husband. The stage is being set. Sometimes, even before an honest conversation can take place, trust is breaking, suspicion is building, and division is occurring. The enemy has now succeeded in theft—stealing a couple's intimacy through division.

• Stage #2: KILL

So now, the wife has no desire for sex due to the growing anger and bitterness she feels toward her husband. The husband grows angry and resentful because his natural desire for sexual intimacy is not being met. He uses these feelings to further justify the need to look at porn. Let me be clear. Women and men can fall prey to porn, but men are more prone to it because of their natural design regarding visual arousal. Both the husband and the wife need help, but the enemy will do all he can to keep them from it. At the same time, he tells the husband, *you don't need help. What guy doesn't sneak a peek now and then?* He tells the wife, *what would your friends really think of you if they knew this was a problem in your marriage?* The couple is now even further apart—emotionally separated from one another and from the help they need. The enemy is well on his way to accomplishing the next goal: killing the marriage in divorce.

• Stage #3: DESTROY

Marriage, God's mirror intended to reflect the relationship between Christ and His church, has been shattered again. Now there are two hurting people, more if children are involved. Depression and oppression set in. The enemy accuses both parties, *if only you weren't such a failure as a husband (or wife), you wouldn't be in this mess. You are beyond help. Things will never be the same again, you might as well just call it quits now.* Sadly, one or both individuals may do so. No matter how it ends, when we fall into the enemy's trap, the collateral damage is immense. The enemy has succeeded in separating two who were one, and has profoundly damaged them and their children, as well as their witness to a watching world. He has gained the upper hand in his goal to destroy them. Tragically, they may have never seen it coming.

Many simply don't believe in the unseen world. They don't take into consideration that evil is constantly coming against them. They blame each other, believe the lies and whispers, and fall prey to their enemy's ultimate goals: division, separation, divorce, and destruction.

The enemy is very good at creating mirages that convince a person that there is something so much better than what they are experiencing, it could be another relationship, a career, a social status. The enemy will use current hardships and help to inflame those emotions to convince a person that they deserve to be happier, to be taken care of better, to have more money…

While pornography is a more obvious form of spiritual attack on a marriage, there are others that are not so overt. Take a look at these strategies that the enemy likes to use to divide and conquer marriages:

Social Media. This is most certainly the modern weaponry of our day often used to separate husbands and wives. Simply spending too much time on these channels can create distance between you and your spouse.

Careers. When both a husband and a wife prioritize their careers over their marriage, it is a recipe for disaster. Mark

10:9 says, "What God has joined together, let no man separate," and I believe this also includes no job, sport, or opportunity. None of these things should trump or get in between the two of you.

Family Members. Parents, siblings, and even children should never be allowed to speak disrespectfully of or come against a spouse. The enemy is looking for ways to divide the two of you and using others is an easy way to do it.

Money. Following money and advancement is an easy trap to fall into. Make sure it does not come between or before the integrity, health, or benefit of your marriage.

Friends. They have their place, but not before the needs and desires of your spouse.

Parenting. The challenges of raising children can weaken a marriage if both spouses are not on the same page, especially with rebellious children. Stay together, set and keep boundaries, and remember that you're on the same team.

Sickness. Whether it's mental, physical, or emotional, sickness can be trying and can lead a spouse to grow weary, become desperate, and even look for a way out. Be on your guard.

The Grass is Greener

Hardships in marriage is the perfect opportunity to create this mentality and mirage that "if only I was married to so and so, or if only I had taken that job, if only I had listened to… my life would be so much better."

Do any of these strategies look familiar? If so, recognize that any issue left unresolved between the two of you will be used by the enemy as a weapon against you and your marriage. If we allow our hearts and minds to go to these unhealthy places, it's only a matter of time before our actions meet them there.

Warfare will continue to be a reality until we are at last with the Lord. As husbands and wives, we must stand in the gap for each other and not allow the enemy to position us against each other. God has made us to overcome. He has given us His Word. He has given us His Spirit. It is He that has already given us the victory!

To Think About: What is the enemy using to divide the two of you? Is he employing any of the strategies mentioned here? Are there any hidden thoughts you are entertaining that are really a mirage? Is there a weak area in your spouse's life where you can come alongside and help in the battle?

Chapter 12
Thank You for Our Tomorrow

This book almost wasn't written. It is a miracle in and of itself because our marriage is.

I remember when we were living in Hawaii, just seven years after we got married. Victor's PTSD was at its worst and our marriage was in bad shape. My heart had grown hard toward him and we flat out just didn't like being around each other. I called a pastor at our church and told him I wanted out. I didn't care about our vows anymore. It was either my way or the highway.

Maybe you find yourself in that same spot right now. Maybe you don't care anymore. Maybe you already have one foot out the door.

Fortunately, the pastor I called told me that leaving Victor was not the right thing to do. He was gentle and understanding, but he was very clear quitting was not the solution. And while I don't know you or your exact situation, I want to encourage you all the same.

Some of the biggest lies the enemy tells a struggling couple are, *Things will never change*, or, *your marriage will always be bad*. Then he targets our emotions by convincing us with another lie, *you don't love your spouse and you never have*, and finishes it off with, *you'd be better off getting a divorce*.

Do any of these sounds familiar? We've heard them all, too.

When we were going through a particularly tough time, I remember reading 2 Corinthians 10:3-5, "For though we walk in the flesh, we do not war according to the flesh. For the weapons of our warfare are not carnal, but mighty in God for pulling down strongholds, casting down arguments and every high thing that exalts itself against the knowledge of God, bringing every thought into captivity to the obedience of Christ." While I didn't fully understand this verse at the time, I believe the Spirit of God gave me enough understanding to see that this battle encompassed more than just the problems Victor and I were having.

When you feel like quitting, remember that it's not just the two of you in the boxing ring. Dark forces are working against you, but you also have God on your side.

The enemy works hard to destroy marriage and unfortunately has plenty of material to work with. For one thing, we live in a culture that says, "just get a divorce." Marriage requires 100% commitment from both parties to make it work. One spouse may have to give more effort than another, for a season. Another reason marriages fail is that we, as a culture, have a short-term view regarding life's challenges. Some couples see no end in sight and give up. Their reaction to temporary hardship causes permanent termination. Others feel trapped and listen to the world's advice instead of seeking godly counsel and practical help to go the distance. Last, there is the "me, myself and I" mentality that leaves no room for the needs of another, much less the daily, long-term effort needed for two to become one. How very sad.

These are our culture's attitudes and lies about marriage that often destroy it from within. More often, though, the reasons why a marriage fails are as personal as the two people in it. The invisible baggage we bring into marriage on the day we say "I do" has to be unpacked and dealt with.

Such was the case with us.

We both had many issues, creating a war zone in our home. Left unaddressed, anger, unforgiveness, shame, guilt, bitterness, and other powerfully destructive emotions will catapult normal disagreements into major explosions. We each had to take an honest, hard look at ourselves to get to the root of the anger inside us.

It was easy for me to look at Victor and see his dysfunction, yet I was blind to my own. It wasn't until he found healing through a long, therapeutic journey that included 123 visits to a multitude of trauma specialists and therapists that I had to finally come to terms with my own issues. I could no longer hide behind Victor's craziness anymore. My problems were now taking center stage and I didn't like it. Now, *I* was the one overreacting, instantaneously going from zero to 10 on the anger chart and displaying ungodly behavior. Though my wounds were very different, I saw the freedom Victor was experiencing and I wanted healing as well.

So many of us carry baggage with us throughout our lives. Wounds that get buried deep into our soul often never see the light of day. They don't evaporate or disappear. Instead, they just get stronger and deeper. Eventually, we pass them off as habits. "This is just how I am," or "I am Irish, and I have an Irish temper," or "This is how my family dealt with things." We tell our spouses, "It's not my fault. I am this way because of what this person did to me." This denial and the accompanying refusal to pursue healing is often what destroys a marriage.

But it doesn't have to be this way. There is hope.

I am so very grateful for the heart and soul counseling that helped heal the wounds of my past and clarify my thinking. If we are willing, we *can* heal from deep wounds. If we are willing, we *can* be free of destructive thought patterns. If we are willing, we *can* confront lies we have believed about ourselves with the truth of God's Word. Once these issues are out in the open, then we can start dealing with our wounds as we journey toward healing.

Marriage is intended to be a beautiful place to deal with life's wounds. It's not easy, but when trust, compassion, and love are nurtured and cultivated, marriage is the healthiest atmosphere in which healing can begin. Ecclesiastes 4:12 speaks of the strength of this bond, "A cord of three strands is not quickly broken." God intended marriage to be that place of strength and security—to weather all of life's challenges, forever.

I want to encourage you to try to see past what you're feeling right now. This is hard to do. Our emotions are very powerful, but don't base your decisions on them. I know your feelings are real, but are they grounded in truth? Are you listening to belittling lies about your spouse or lies that tell you that you can do better? Are you listening to a lie that says you don't need him or that marriage was a mistake?

Every marriage has issues that need to be discussed. Make them a priority and pray over them. Ask God to help you and be present in your discussions. Ask the Holy Spirit to soften your heart, as well as your spouse's heart, so that they can receive what you have to say. Ask the Holy Spirit to show you when to speak about these things. Timing is important; when we are tired, hungry, or stressed, we are already resistant to tough conversations. Picture yourself talking to your spouse and hear yourself speak. Can you speak with gentleness in your tone? Can you speak with humility? Can you say what you need to say without loaded accusations? People hear us better when we are thoughtful with our words and delivery. Your spouse is no exception.

I want to encourage you with something that encouraged me when we were going through some of our greatest challenges: This will not last forever. It's a simple truth, but when times were hard and I thought that what we were going through was much more than I could handle, I needed to be reminded of this. We were able to get through those seemingly impossible moments. Looking back, they were just that—moments. Those hard times did in fact end. Yours will too.

Thank goodness we not only grow older, but wiser, too, as we submit to the Lord. Today, I see Victor not only as my husband, but also as my brother in Christ. He's not perfect and neither am I. He makes mistakes. So do I. Grace for one another is what makes all the difference.

Marriage is similar to endurance training. Though you will experience pain as you grow, you will get stronger and stronger. We often forget that marriage is supposed to have struggles. You are two people with different thoughts, ideas, and backgrounds. You *should* be seeing things differently. I love what Ruth Graham said, "If both of you agree on everything, one of you is not needed."

Embrace your differences. Learn to appreciate them. Pray through the issues that need addressing. Endure and get stronger together.

Persevering through hard times creates an unmatched oneness and provides such wonderful joy when you look back on your journey together. The places where you are weak as a couple can become a mighty fortress. Through the power of Christ, the two of you can become a force to be reckoned with, one that others will admire. Your testimony of endurance will not be in vain. You are teaching your children a lifetime of lessons as they watch you endure these hardships. Remember, one day, they too will go through hard times in their own marriages. It's okay. It will not destroy them to see your imperfections and humanness. In fact, it will make them stronger. They will see and know that you did not give up.

There are days when I look at Victor and think to myself, "This has all been worth it." Often, this thought comes in the midst of everyday things like shopping, having a conversation, driving somewhere in the car, sitting side-by-side, or while I'm listening to him speak at an event. Other times, life's big moments are when that thought hits me hard. Recently, I saw my husband holding our beautiful granddaughter. His eyes lit up just looking at her precious face. Oh, my goodness. My heart leaped inside of me. Through our baby, God gave us this beautiful grandbaby, for whom we both have such unbelievable love. My heart was full of joy.

The same thought came as I watched Victor officiate our son's wedding. I was overwhelmed watching him speak life over our son, knowing what marriage is truly about. He looked into our son's eyes, man-to-man, and encouraged him to build a godly marriage. None of this would have been possible if we had given up. All I could say was, "God, thank you. Thank you for keeping us when we didn't know what tomorrow held. Thank you for keeping us when we had nothing, and our hearts were hardened against one another. You knew what our tomorrow held. Thank you!"

To Think About: What baggage did you bring into your marriage? Are there issues that still need to be addressed? What lies has the enemy been telling you about your marriage? How can you counter those with God's truth? If there are conversations you need to have with your spouse, pray that the Holy Spirit would lead you in those moments and for God's peace in your marriage.

Chapter 13
The Fruit of the Fight

We often stand in awe of how God continues to grow the fruit of our commitment to one another—in us as individuals, in our children, and in our ministry—in spite of ourselves.

He is so good.

Ministry Through Trauma Films

One of the ways God uses us to reach wounded people is through the power of film. The brutal aftereffects of trauma that Victor endured, as well as his misdiagnosis of bi-polar disorder, caused us to wonder if others were experiencing the same things. How many were unable to connect the dots of yesterday's trauma to today's unexplained behaviors? How many had been misdiagnosed with a mental illness or other psychiatric disorders, without considering the possibility of past trauma?

When we learned that as many as 22 veterans take their own lives every day due to PTSD, we knew we had to do something to reach them with a message of hope. In 2014, after we made "The Victor Marx Story: When Impossible is the Only Way Out," we saw a great need to help people who suffer from PTSD. We started the filming process and made our first documentary, a film about PTSD called "Triggered." The response was overwhelming. It was shown at the Pentagon, and a general there said "Triggered" should be shown on every Army base around the world. We are currently working with retired officers who are passionate about getting this much-needed film into the hands of those who need it within the military community.

Sadly, trauma is not limited to veterans. It is a part of life. For some, it is a one-time event that is more easily processed and overcome. For others, it is complex and life altering. It is not always easy to recognize its effects, and treating it takes time and persistence. When severe trauma happens, many areas of the human body are affected simultaneously. Oftentimes, the brain stores the trauma and can bury it deep within, sending the individual into survival mode. When left unaddressed, though, stressors in everyday life can trigger responses that surface much later in unwanted behavior. Many civilians struggle with PTSD as well, so we made a second documentary called "Triggered Too."

A father of four saw this film and was finally able to understand why his wife just up and left him. The trauma of her childhood abuse had surfaced, and being a wife and mom felt like more than she could handle. This is just one of the many heartbreaking stories we hear of how PTSD affects people from all walks of life. Some have been able, for the first time, to put a name to their struggle. Others made the important step of seeking help for themselves or for their families. Still more have become aware of this serious condition that affects so many worldwide. These films are a powerful way to let those who are struggling know that they are not alone, and that help is available.

Ministry to Broken Marriages

One of our favorite things about doing ministry together is sharing what we have learned about marriage at conferences or when we are interviewed by the media. We pray our story will encourage others to stay the course, knowing that all things are truly possible in Him.

I have learned so much about what it means to love my husband and to be his wife, in the way that God intended for me when he designed marriage. If I were speaking to a newlywed wife today, my advice would be:

Look at your husband as your brother in Christ. Know that he's human and that he will fail you. He has a lifetime to figure you out. Let it take that long. The longer you are married, the more you learn of each other and the more you grow together as one. Strive to be your husband's greatest ally in all areas of his life. Let him know that no matter what challenges the two of you face, you can have the hard conversations and you will still be his no matter what. If he comes to you and shares that he was tempted by lustful thoughts or an advance by a coworker, show him that you will not be shaken. Do not respond with jealousy, anger, or accusations, but rather, look at him as a man, a man not above temptation. Be his wife. Be his prayer warrior.

If you are in a place where your husband has abandoned you emotionally, mentally and even physically, understand that it is a much deeper issue. This could be a spiritual issue that must be dealt with spiritual weapons. If your spouse has departed in any of these areas, chances are he has departed from God. As difficult as it can be, don't take it personal. Stop looking at it as a personal attack on you, but rather understand that it is between God and your spouse. The enemy is going to town trying hard to destroy your spouse and your marriage. Stand in the gap in prayer. Allow God to do the work in him, don't interfere and try to stop the pain and consequences of his choices or behavior. Be his ally with strong and practical boundaries. It will be a protective hedge against the enemy, and as he seeks to destroy your marriage, your marriage will only grow stronger in years to come.

Our choices today affect future generations. Our children are the greatest evidence of this truth, and that should strengthen us for when hard times come to pass.

As I write this now, my soul is so grateful, and my eyes fill up with tears as I look back and see just how good our God was and is. We didn't give up. Neither one of us did. Had we done so, we would not be experiencing the joy of seeing our children marry or have the incredible blessing of seeing, holding, and loving our first and now second grandchild—together. We have so much history of God's goodness in our marriage and family that those moments of trial and challenge were just that, moments.

Life on earth is hard and it's unfair to so many. Even through incredible hardships, God has given us so many wonderful things on this journey. Next to our salvation and relationship with Him, the greatest gift we've been given is that of marriage. He knew life would be better walking as husband and wife—together—through all the cycles and situations of life. He knew what He was doing when He said, "It is not good for man to be alone."

We often talk about our future and how we look forward to growing old together. We see ourselves continuing to minister to the traumatized, here in the United States and over in Iraq, Syria and Cambodia. Looking back, all we can really say is, "Thank you, God! Thank you for being so faithful to us and for bringing us through very dark times. Thank you for giving us the faith we needed to hold on to one another and believe that we would get through." God helped us even when it felt like the enemy was taking over, and we thought would might lose it all.

When we are finished here, we desire to leave behind evidence of God's goodness and faithfulness in our lives: our marriage, our children, grandchildren, and the ministry He called us to. We made it through many challenges, but also enjoyed much victory and success. Learning to surrender our own limited ideas of what marriage is about and truly grasp God's idea and incredible plan that He put in place for marriage from the beginning of time has brought sweeter rewards and greater satisfaction than we could have ever imagined. We can look back knowing that we lived our best, we loved our best, we forgave, we were forgiven, and although we were imperfectly one, we were one.

To Think About: What legacy do you and your spouse desire to leave behind with regards to your marriage? What do you want your children and grandchildren to remember you for? Take some time to discuss and write out what that looks like.

These are three more reasons why I am so glad we didn't give up — our three older children on their wedding days.

To listen to Eileen's Podcast

With a heart to engage with women on the reality of life — the good, the bad and the not so flattering ... Eileen will explore all things women. Discussing issues all women face with truth, reality and rawness, Eileen will cover topics like marriage, parenting, emotions, health and spirituality. Join Eileen and special guests as they explore the God-given influence women have in the world.

LISTEN ON ANY PODCAST APP
BY SEARCHING "EILEEN MARX"

ALL THINGS POSSIBLE.

ALL THINGS POSSIBLE EXISTS TO IDENTIFY,
INTERRUPT & RESTORE THOSE AFFECTED BY
TRAUMA. WE REGULARLY PLACE OURSELVES IN
HARM'S WAY TO REACH AND RESTORE VICTIMS
OF TRAUMA. OUR ONGOING EFFORTS HAVE
HELPED THOUSANDS OF CHILDREN, WOMEN
AND MEMBERS OF OUR MILITARY DISCOVER NEW
HOPE, EXPERIENCE LASTING CHANGE AND
RECEIVE ONGOING SUPPORT.

VICTORMARX.COM

VICTOR MARX LEADERSHIP & TRAINING CENTER

The vision of the Victor Marx Leadership & Training Center in collaboration with All Things Possible Ministries is to train and equip a new generation of spiritual leaders for the mission field, the workplace and the home. We endeavor to see strong families being built, marriages flourish and every man, woman and young person we serve grow closer in their relationship with Jesus Christ — and to be prepared every step of the way.

LEARN MORE:
VICTORMARX.COM/TRAINING

TRIGGERED

A groundbreaking new film chronicling the struggles of PTSD recovery and healing as told through a series of interviews.

Our Military Heroes fight for our freedom and many times come back having to fight for their own mental freedom. Triggered helps to explain the battle going on inside the mind and provides simple tools how you can be free from so many devastating affects and behaviors that can develop from the trauma experienced.

TRIGGERED TOO (for civilians)

Trauma or PTSD is part of our world. It's not prejudiced nor discriminating and it can take down even the strongest of minds. Give yourself and those you love a chance to heal and get past the anxiety, panic attacks, depression and many more debilitating emotions and reactions.

VICTORMARX.COM/TRIGGERED